PianoLab

An Introduction to Class Piano

PianoLab

An Introduction to Class Piano

Third Edition

Carolynn A. Lindeman

San Francisco State University

 Wadsworth Publishing Company

I(T)P™ An International Thomson Publishing Company

Belmont • Albany • Bonn • Boston • Cincinnati • Detroit • London • Madrid • Melbourne •
Mexico City • New York • Paris • San Francisco • Singapore • Tokyo • Toronto • Washington

Music Editor: Katherine Hartlove
Editorial Assistant: Jessica Monday
Production Services Coordinator: Debby Kramer
Production: Greg Hubit Bookworks
Print Buyer: Barbara Britton
Permissions Editor: Robert Kauser

Designer: Wendy LaChance/By Design
Copy Editor: Carole Crouse
Autographer: Ernie Mansfield
Cover Designer: Ark Stein / The Visual Group
Compositor: TBH/Typecast
Printer: Malloy Lithographing, Inc.

For more information, contact Wadsworth Publishing Company:

Wadsworth Publishing Company
10 Davis Drive
Belmont, California 94002, USA

International Thomson Publishing Europe
Berkshire House 168-173
High Holborn
London, WC1V 7AA, England

Thomas Nelson Australia
102 Dodds Street
South Melbourne 3205
Victoria, Australia

Nelson Canada
1120 Birchmount Road
Scarborough, Ontario
Canada M1K 5G4

International Thomson Editores
Campos Eliseos 385, Piso 7
Col. Polanco
11560 México D.F. México

International Thomson Publishing GmbH
Königswinterer Strasse 418
53227 Bonn, Germany

International Thomson Publishing Asia
221 Henderson Road
#05-10 Henderson Building
Singapore 0315

International Thomson Publishing Japan
Hirakawacho Kyowa Building, 3F
2-2-1 Hirakawacho
Chiyoda-ku, Tokyo 102, Japan

Library of Congress Cataloging-in-Publication Data

Lindeman, Carolynn A.
    PianoLab : an introduction to class piano / Carolynn A. Lindeman.
    — 3rd ed.
        p.   cm.
    Includes bibliographical references.
    ISBN 0-534-25140-4
    1. Piano — Methods — Group instruction. 2. Music — Theory,
Elementary. 3. Piano music. I. Title.
MT222.L695   1996
786.2'193 — dc20   95-23956

CONTENTS

Chapter Four 65

Chapter Five   87

Chapter Eight 149

Chapter Nine   *179*

Appendixes   *311*

PREFACE

PianoLab: An Introduction to Class Piano, Third Edition, like the editions that preceded it, was created mindful of the challenges faced by students and their instructors in most class piano courses. Students want to play the piano as quickly as possible and often become frustrated when their physical skills do not keep pace with their conceptual skills. Their varying backgrounds, motivation, and cognitive and psychomotor skills make it impossible for everyone to learn at the same rate. Even with the best facilities, the instructor faces a limited time frame in which to teach the piano basics. It may take one or two quarters or semesters for students to learn their "keyboard geography" and become comfortable at the piano. Add to that the desire to give students more than just a brush with music concepts, and there is indeed a great deal to accomplish in a short time.

These challenges, however, are not insurmountable. Assuming that students have no prior background in music, *PianoLab*, Third Edition, focuses on teaching them to *perform*. And it goes a step further; it gives students an *understanding* of music that they can take with them, regardless of whether they continue to play the piano. Each chapter includes brief materials to develop understanding of the elements of music: melody, rhythm, harmony, and form. Students are then encouraged to apply that knowledge through performance, analysis, improvisation, transposition, harmonization, and composition.

Organization of the Book

The main focus of each chapter is the development of skills and technique. Chapter 1 invites students to explore the keyboard by *making music and creating music* before learning to read it. Subsequent chapters build on that initial exploration through the following:

A wide variety of *playing materials* (over 200), representing art music of the eighteenth through the twentieth centuries by male and female composers, indeterminate music, folk songs, piano blues, boogie-woogie, ragtime, and popular music.

Careful *grading of selections* from the simplest to the more challenging.

Development of music-reading and playing skills simultaneously through exercises and playing materials.

Composing and improvising projects to encourage and develop creativity.

Technique exercises covering skills encountered within each chapter and those to come in subsequent chapters.

End-of-chapter evaluations for students and instructors to evaluate skill development and progress in musical understanding before moving ahead to the next chapter.

Additional Features

PianoLab, Third Edition, also includes a Supplementary Music section with more than fifty selections of solo classical piano pieces; blues, boogie, and ragtime; traditional folk and patriotic songs with piano accompaniment; and folk and popular melodies.

Ensemble pieces are presented in a special section following the Supplementary Music section. These pieces are arranged for two or more players and reflect a variety of styles.

Several appendixes on such topics as musical terms and signs, fingerings for major and minor scales, primary chords in root position and in I–IV$_4^6$–V$_5^6$ position, accompaniment patterns, information on electronic keyboards, a Timeline of Western Art Music and History, a Timeline of Selected Keyboard Composers and Keyboard Instruments, and Biographical Sketches of *PianoLab* Composers help to answer student questions and provide references for study, practice, and review. Following the appendixes is a Glossary of musical terms.

In addition to the subject index, *PianoLab*, Third Edition, has several specialized indexes to provide flexibility and ease of use.

PianoLab stresses strong student orientation, from the Note to Students through each chapter, where a variety of music is offered to help students acquire needed skills and concepts.

An authentic presentation of eighteenth- through twentieth-century music is an important feature of the text. Selections appear in original (*urtext*) edition with only fingerings added. Since few dynamic, tempo, or articulation markings were included in eighteenth-century music, performance notes are often provided (or occasional markings are placed in parentheses), but no editing is added by the author.

Root-position chords are introduced before chord inversions to solidify student understanding of chord building. Although only the primary chords (in root position and all inversions) are stressed, several examples in the Supplementary Songs sections include secondary chords (also, Appendix F identifies primary and secondary chords in major and minor keys).

Acknowledgments

Creating the third edition of *PianoLab* required the help and support of many people. I am particularly grateful to:

My colleagues and students in the San Francisco State University Music Department for their help in developing, improving, and critiquing *PianoLab* in its various stages.

Composers and friends Nancy Van de Vate, Herbert Bielawa, and Emma Lou Diemer for creating pieces especially for *PianoLab*.

Colleague and friend Dee Spencer for her special arrangements and help with the electronic keyboard section.

Keyboard and performance practices specialist Sandra Soderlund for her critical assessment and review of the Technique Exercises and musical examples and her expert advice on eighteenth-century keyboard performance practices.

Serra High School music instructor James Jordan for his help in preparing the Biographical Sketches of *PianoLab* Composers and the information on electronic keyboards.

Judy Fendell for her research and assistance in preparing the Timeline of Selected Keyboard Composers and Keyboard Instruments.

The following reviewers for their thoughtful and critical comments: Peggy Gorham, City College of San Francisco; Mary Scanlan, Grand Rapids Junior College; Rebecca Shockley, University of Minnesota; and Joan Stubbe, San Jose State University.

Finally, my husband, Al, and son, David, for their love, understanding, and help in making *PianoLab* become a reality.

NOTE TO STUDENTS

About the Book

PianoLab, Third Edition, is designed for you, the beginning student. It assumes no background in music but does assume you have a genuine interest in learning to play the piano and learning about music. As you learn to read and play, you will discover that reading notes and playing scales and chord progressions are not enough. You must also develop an understanding of how music is put together, how it "works," and how rhythm, melody, and harmony interrelate to form musical compositions. This musical understanding evolves mainly through performance but also through analysis, improvisation, transposition, harmonization, and composition. Helping you develop these keyboard skills and music concepts is the goal of *PianoLab*.

Although *PianoLab*, Third Edition, includes more than 200 pieces of music, you do not need to learn all the music to acquire essential concepts and skills. Each chapter includes a number of musical examples for you to perform. Study several of these pieces and use the others, if you wish, for sightreading and extra practice.

Over twenty of the musical selections are arranged to be played in ensembles. The ensemble pieces may be performed with one or two students per piano or with students playing one part and the instructor the other. Parts can also be divided and doubled among students. For individual practice, you can record one part or use a tape recording of the part, then perform the other with the recording.

As you explore the playing examples in the text, you will find that music of all styles and eras, from classical music of the eighteenth through twentieth centuries to popular music, is included. All the music in *PianoLab*, Third Edition, is presented in original form. In the case of eighteenth-century music, this means that only pitches and rhythm are notated; eighteenth-century composers included few tempo, dynamic, and articulation markings in their manuscripts. Since only fingerings have been added to the eighteenth-century pieces, a few performance guidelines to remember for many pieces are these: Play *non legato* (not connected), *mezzo forte* (medium loud), and *moderato* (moderate tempo).

All musical terms and signs, such as *legato*, *mezzo forte*, and *moderato*, are presented in Appendix A, and information about the composers is contained in the Biographical Sketches of *PianoLab* Composers. In addition, you can place the composers and their music in the appropriate historical period by utilizing the Timeline of Western Art Music and History and the Timeline of Selected Keyboard Composers and Keyboard Instruments.

Suggestions for Practice

Certainly every beginning pianist needs to devote time outside of class to practice in order to progress and to develop skills. Reserve a particular time each day for this purpose. (A little work each day is better than a longer practice session a couple of days a week.) Here are some suggestions for your practice session:

1. Begin with several Technique Exercises. The Technique Exercises at the end of each chapter are simple patterns that can be memorized so you can direct all your attention to seeing and feeling the correct hand and finger positions and listening for good tone production.

2. Visually analyze each piece before playing to get a "picture" of the piece. Look to see how fast or how slowly the piece should be performed. Are there any changes in louds and softs? Does the piece break into easily recognizable parts? Notice how the melody moves up and down and repeats. Check the meter signature, the kinds of notes and rests, and any particular rhythmic patterns. Are chords outlined in the right- and left-hand parts? Look up all tempo and dynamic terms in Appendix A. Check information on the composer and his or her place in history in the Biographical Sketches of *PianoLab* Composers and the two timelines.

3. Practice new and old pieces in several different ways. Review the keyboard position(s). Perform just the rhythm of the piece. Perform the piece slowly hands together, listening carefully. Practice hands separately, in small sections, and so on. Always evaluate your playing. Practice problem spots slowly. Repeat until you are satisfied with your performance.

4. End your practice session by improvising a bit at the keyboard. Create music using ideas and composing projects found in the chapters or by applying your own ideas.

Class Piano and You

As you study the piano in a group setting, you will find that beginning pianists progress at different rates of speed. Some in your class will develop eye and hand coordination quickly and almost effortlessly. Others will work diligently and slowly to achieve the same results in a much longer period of time. These individual differences are always present in the mastery of a new technical skill, whether it be sports or piano playing. However, although beginning pianists develop the physical skills at different rates, most adults develop music concepts at a similar rate. Be aware that your physical and conceptual skills may not keep pace with each other. Try to understand this phenomenon and do not become frustrated by it. Most of all, your progress and pleasure in piano study depend on you. You must make the personal commitment and accept the challenge of learning a new skill. It is hoped that *PianoLab*, Third Edition, and the music course in which you are enrolled will help you meet those challenges and "turn you on" to the exciting world of music.

Grand piano by Johann Schmidt, Salzburg, Austria, 1788 (Smithsonian Institution photo no. 303,536. Used by permission.)

THE PIANO

Historical Development

Bartolommeo Cristofori is credited with inventing the piano about 1709 in Florence, Italy. The piano differed from the earlier keyboard instruments, the clavichord and the harpsichord, in that its hammer action could provide continuous gradations of loud and soft tones. Cristofori's name for his invention was *gravicembalo col piano e forte* ("harpsichord with soft and loud"). The instrument, however, came to be known as the *pianoforte* or the abbreviated name *piano*. (A Timeline of Selected Keyboard Composers and Keyboard Instruments is located in Appendix L.)

Grand piano (with the courtesy
of Yamaha Corporation of
America, California, and
Yamaha Corporation, Japan)

Upright piano (Steinway and Sons.
Used by permission.)

Electronic piano lab (Courtesy of Young Chang/Kurzweil.)

Although the piano was invented in the early part of the eighteenth century, it did not become widely used until the latter part of the century. In the nineteenth century, it went through numerous improvements that ultimately resulted in our present-day grand piano.

The upright piano was an innovation of the nineteenth century, and with this smaller and more economical instrument, pianos became a fixture in many American and European homes. In fact, it is said that in the 1850s there were more pianos than bathtubs in the United States, and in the early 1900s more pianos than telephones in the home.

Today pianos still come in the two eighteenth- and nineteenth-century shapes—the grand and the upright; also in recent years upright electronic pianos have been developed. Because the sound can be channeled through headphones, the electronic pianos are often used in a group piano setting.

For information on electronic keyboards (basic keyboards, digital pianos, and synthesizers), see the section Electronic Keyboards in Appendix J.

The Instrument

An acoustic piano produces its sound by strings being struck by hammers, which are put into action by the keys. The complex mechanism connecting this key–hammer motion is called the piano's *action*. The small but long pieces of felt-covered wood that lie above the strings are called the *dampers*. They move up and down with the action via connecting wires. The dampers allow the strings to vibrate freely the moment the hammer strikes and stop the vibration when the key is released.

A standard-size piano *keyboard* has eighty-eight keys: fifty-two white and thirty-six black keys. Some electronic pianos have shorter keyboards.

The modern piano has two or three foot-operated **pedals:** the **soft pedal** to the left, the **sostenuto pedal** in the middle, and the **damper pedal** to the right. Some upright pianos have only the soft and damper pedals. The damper pedal is used to connect and sustain tones, whereas the soft pedal, called **una corda** ("one string") **pedal,** is used to reduce the volume of sound. The sostenuto pedal (on a grand piano) permits the sustaining of a chord or a single note with the pedal while the hand is free to play other notes.

ELEMENTS OF MUSIC: MELODY, RHYTHM, HARMONY, AND FORM

Although a pianist must develop skills in playing and reading music, he or she must also understand basic concepts about music. Music concepts may be studied within the framework of the elements of music. Most music of Western cultures contains four elements: melody, rhythm, harmony, and form. An individual element may be studied by itself; however, melody, rhythm, harmony, and form seldom occur singularly in music. Rather, they are combined and interrelated to form musical compositions. Using the song "Norwegian Wood" as an example, one can explore how the elements of music are combined and interrelated to form a composition. (The instructor should perform this song to illustrate the elements of music.)

Norwegian Wood (This Bird Has Flown)

John Lennon (England, 1940–1980)
Paul McCartney (England, b. 1942)

(Instructor part)

I looked a - round and I no - ticed there was - n't a chair.

And when I a - woke, I was a - lone, this bird had flown;

So I lit a fire, Is - n't it good Nor - we - gian wood?

Melody

A **melody** *is a linear succession of sounds (pitches) and silences moving through time— that is, the horizontal structure of music.* Each melody is a unique combination of sounds and silences, which, when organized in a series, creates a sense of line or a meaningful musical shape.

Pitches in a melody may move up or down or remain the same. Listen to a performance of the melody of "Norwegian Wood." Notice how the melody moved up and down and often repeats. Connect the pitches on the score to discover the melodic **contour.**

Melodic contour

"Norwegian Wood" is distinctive not only for its pitches and resultant contour but also for its rhythm.

Rhythm

Rhythm *refers to all the durations of sounds and silences that occur in music as well as the organization of these sounds and silences in time.* Perhaps the most fundamental ingredient of rhythm is the **beat** or pulse. When we listen to music, we often respond to the beat by tapping our feet "in time." The beat is that underlying pulsation that one feels recurring steadily as music moves through time. First, clap or tap the steady beat while "Norwegian Wood" is performed. Then, during a second performance, mark the beats under the music like this:

Sounds and silences in a melody move through time with a beat or, more often, in longer or shorter durations than the beat. If you clap just the **rhythm of the melody** for "Norwegian Wood," these longer and shorter durations will be obvious.

Harmony

The simultaneous sounding of two or more tones not only gives the melody support and color but also defines the melody itself. **Harmony** *is the vertical structure of music that moves through time and supports the melody.*

Chords are the principal building blocks of harmony. Chords include at least three pitches sounded simultaneously. On the piano, chords are generally played with the left hand (in the lower register), while melody is performed with the right hand (in the middle to upper register). (In popular music, chords are often indicated by an uppercase letter above the staff.) Locate the letter names of the chords in "Norwegian Wood," and listen to a performance with chords added to the melody.

Form

The overall design, plan, or order of a musical composition is known as its **form.** Musical ideas expressed with pitches and rhythms are organized by the composer in various ways to create artistic balance. Usually, smaller units of musical ideas are put together to create larger ones until finally an overall form or total piece of music emerges.

Music, as well as other art forms, utilizes unity and variety to achieve aesthetic balance. A brief musical idea called a **motive** is often used as the smallest unit to unify an entire composition. The recurring rhythmic motive in "Norwegian Wood" is:

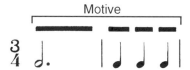

If a motive may be likened to a few words in a speech, a **phrase** corresponds to a clause or a simple sentence. As "Norwegian Wood" is performed, decide where the phrases begin and end; then mark the phrases with brackets. Notice which phrases are alike and which are different.

Just as motives are put together to build longer units called phrases, so phrases are combined to build still longer units known as **sections.** Some compositions have two or three sections, and others go beyond to create an extended sectional form.

SUMMARY

To play the piano intelligently and sensitively, one must develop basic keyboard skills and understand basic concepts about melody, rhythm, harmony, and form. This preliminary discussion was simply an introduction to the elements of music. Each chapter in *PianoLab* focuses on various music concepts within these elements. The Timeline of Western Art Music and History (Appendix K) includes the specific characteristics of the elements of music from the Middle Ages to the present day.

Playing Position
Key Names
Finger Numbers
Improvisation
Drones, Ostinati
Indeterminate Music

POSITION AT THE KEYBOARD

Sit directly in front of the middle of the keyboard, with feet flat on the floor. The manufacturer's label can be used as a reference on most pianos. Sit far enough back from the keyboard so that your arms can move freely and your body bends slightly forward at the waist. The piano bench should be high enough so that your elbows are at keyboard level.

Playing Position

Drop your arms to your sides in a dangling position. Your arms should hang loosely from the shoulders. Keeping that same relaxed position, lift your hands to the keyboard. Rest your fingers on the keys. Notice that your hands are slightly arched, your fingers are gently curved, and your wrists are straight. The wrists should be level with the keys. Always try to retain that relaxed position with arched hands, curved fingers, and wrists straight but flexible. If you should begin to feel tense while playing, stop playing and drop your arms to your side in the dangling, relaxed position. Then begin again.

Hand Position

Your hands should stay as motionless as possible. Retain a natural rounded hand shape and keep your fingers as close to the keys as possible. Keys should be "struck," not pressed. As you strike (do not push) the keys, your hands should not move up and down with the fingers. Remember to play each key with the fleshy

Correct position at the keyboard

Correct hand position

part of the finger. Fingernails must be short. As you play, your eyes should not be on the keys; rather, develop a "feel" for the keys—play by touch.

Finger Numbers

The arabic numbers 1–5 are assigned to specific fingers of both hands. These numbers (usually written very small) appear above or below the notes in piano music to indicate the preferred fingering.

Finger numbers

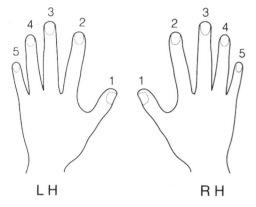

LH   RH

Finger numbers in music

Unison Melody 3 (excerpt)
(from *Mikrokosmos*, Vol. 1)

Béla Bartók (Hungary, 1881–1945)

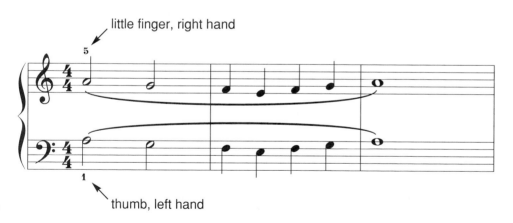

EXPLORING THE KEYBOARD

Pitches go higher as your fingers move to the right on the keyboard and lower as you move to the left.

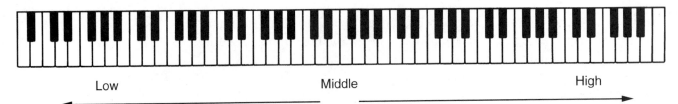

Low   Middle   High

1. The black keys alternate in groups of twos and threes up and down the keyboard. Find two black keys together in the middle of the keyboard. Using your right-hand (RH) index finger (2) and middle finger (3), play these two keys moving up the keyboard (both keys at once).

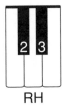
RH

2. Using your left-hand (LH) index finger (2) and middle finger (3), find two black keys together in the middle of the keyboard. Play these two keys moving down the keyboard (both keys at once).

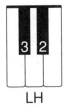
LH

3. Find three black keys together in the lowest part of the keyboard. Play these three keys with your left-hand index (2), middle (3), and ring (4) fingers moving up to the middle of the keyboard (one key at a time). With your right hand, begin with the three black keys at the highest part of the keyboard and play these keys moving down to the middle (one key at a time).

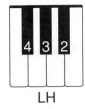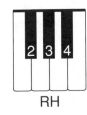
LH   RH

NAMES OF THE WHITE KEYS

The first seven letters of the alphabet are used to identify the white keys. This alphabetical pattern proceeds from left to right.

Keyboard Landmarks

Two keys, C and F, may be used as landmarks for identifying and learning the names of keys. **Middle C,** the C closest to the middle of the keyboard, is a focal point for beginning piano instruction.

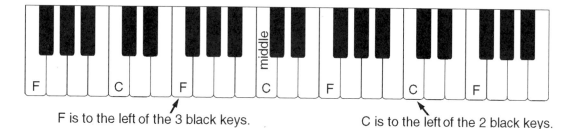

F is to the left of the 3 black keys.   C is to the left of the 2 black keys.

Keyboard Practice—White Keys

1. Locate and play every C on the keyboard; then play every F.

2. Start with the lowest white key and play up the keyboard, saying the names as you play. Change fingers so that you use them all. Reverse the naming by starting with the highest white key and playing downward, again saying the names of the keys as you play.

3. Locate and play the following pitches as quickly as you can.

a high D	the lowest A	middle C
a low G	the highest F	the A above middle C
an E in the middle	a B in the middle	the G below middle C

Keyboard Practice—Finger Numbers

1. Practice saying the finger numbers aloud and moving the correct finger up and down.

2. As finger numbers are called out, play the correct fingers "in the air." Practice first with separate hands, then hands together.

3. At the keyboard, rest both hands on the pitches G, A, B, C, and D.

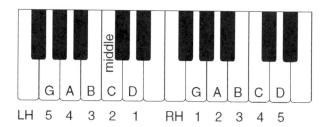

LH 5 4 3 2 1   RH 1 2 3 4 5

As someone plays and calls out finger numbers in rhythm, echo by playing correct fingers (and keys).

Examples: Instructor: Students:

5	5	5	5	5	5	5	5
1	11	1	1	1	11	1	1
33	3	3	3	33	3	3	3

4. Try to play a melody such as Beethoven's "Ode to Joy" (p. 67) dictated with finger numbers.

Playing the White Keys

1. With your left hand (LH), practice the following blues progression with correct fingering. Hold each key for four steady beats. When you are secure with the bass line, another player (or other players) can perform "Emily's Blues" on p. 218 with you.

Blues progression (students)

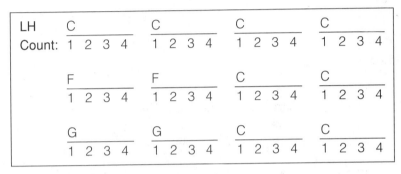

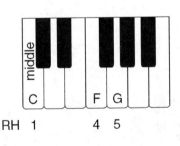

2. Play the following blues progression with your right hand (RH) in the middle register of the piano. Check for correct fingering. Again, hold each key for four steady beats. While you play this higher part, another player (or other players) can perform "Boogie Rock," p. 151.

Blues progression (students)

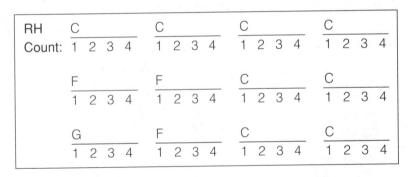

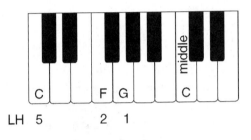

Other pieces that may be performed with this blues progression are on pp. 135, 136, 139, 150, and 255.

SHARPS AND FLATS

The keys immediately to the left and right of the white keys are identified as sharps (♯) and flats (♭).

Sharps: Move one key up (right) to the nearest black or white key.

Flats: Move one key down (left) to the nearest black or white key.

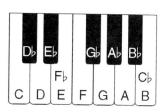

NAMES OF THE BLACK KEYS

Each black key has two names. For example, the black key between A and B is called A♯ or B♭. A♯ and B♭ are referred to as **enharmonics.**

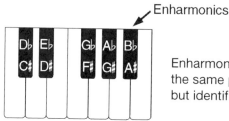

Enharmonics

Enharmonics are tones sounding
the same pitch or key on the keyboard
but identified by different letter names.

Keyboard Practice—Black Keys

1. Locate the black keys by touch. Find black-key groupings; then play and name individual black keys.
2. Start with the lowest black key and play the black keys up the keyboard, saying the sharp names as you play. Repeat, saying the flat names for each key.
3. Locate and play the following pitches as quickly as you can.

a high D♯	the highest E♭	the f♯ above middle C
a low G♭	the lowest C♯	a high A♭
an A♯ in the middle	a D♭ in the middle	the B♭ below middle C

Keyboard Practice—Sharps and Flats

1. Locate and play the black-key sharps; then play the white-key sharps.
2. Locate and play the black-key flats; then play the white-key flats.

3. Play the following accompaniment line with correct fingering. This part will fit with Leopold Mozart's "Minuet" (p. 228). Hold each pitch for three steady beats. 𝄆 𝄇 are *repeat signs*, indicating that the pitches between the signs should be repeated.

"Minuet" (students)

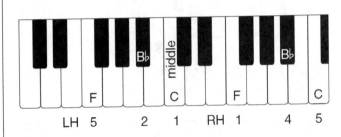

RH 𝄆 F	F	B♭	B♭
Count: 1 2 3	1 2 3	1 2 3	1 2 3
F	F	C	F 𝄇
1 2 3	1 2 3	1 2 3	1 2 3
LH 𝄆 C	C	C	C
1 2 3	1 2 3	1 2 3	1 2 3
F	F	C	F 𝄇
1 2 3	1 2 3	1 2 3	1 2 3

Improvisation—Black Keys

The black keys are an excellent place to begin **improvisation,** or music performed extemporaneously. As you create different melodies and accompaniments, you will find that practically everything blends well.

1. With your LH, play F♯ and C♯ simultaneously on the lower part of the keyboard. Repeat this drone over and over in a steady rhythm. (A **drone** may be two tones sounded together and repeated over and over.)

Drone: C♯ ⎤
(LH)   F♯ ⎦

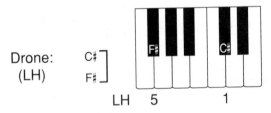

Then try an ostinato with your RH. (An **ostinato** is a continuous repetition of a melodic or rhythmic pattern.) Repeat over and over an ostinato using C♯ and A♯ in the middle of the keyboard. Try playing in this short, short, short, short, long rhythm.

Ostinato: C♯ C♯ C♯ C♯ A♯ _____
(RH)

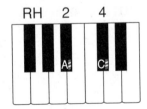

Finally, perform the LH drone and the RH ostinato together. Repeat over and over in a steady rhythm. As soon as the two-hand part is coordinated, another player (or other players) can improvise melodies on the black keys with the drone-ostinato as an accompaniment.

RH: ⁴C♯   C♯   C♯   C♯   A♯ _____

LH: ₁ C♯ ⌉
      ₅ F♯ ⌋

Then try the drone in the RH and the ostinato in the LH.

RH: ₅ C♯ ⌉
      ₁ F♯ ⌋

LH: C♯   C♯   C♯   C♯   A♯ _____
        ₂

2. By yourself, try playing the F♯–C♯ drone with your LH and improvising on any of the black keys with your RH. Keep the LH part steady. In the beginning, if you have trouble playing two different things, try matching the RH playing with the LH steady rhythm part. Then gradually experiment with your RH moving more freely on the black keys. Finally, try the drone with the RH and improvise with the LH.

3. Improvise in the boogie-woogie style. One pianist or group of pianists should set up the following **boogie-woogie** bass in the lower register. The pitches can be distributed between the two hands. "Walk" up and down the keys without stopping.

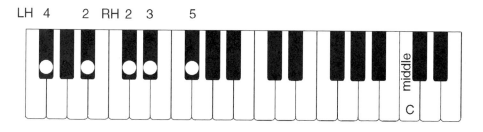

When the walking bass is secure, a second pianist or group of pianists should join in playing the same black keys but in the middle register and simultaneously in a slower rhythm. One idea would be to play the pitches at the beginning of each walking bass pattern.

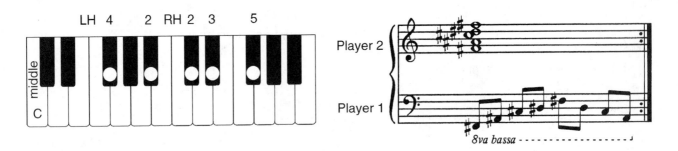

When these two parts are secure, a third pianist can improvise on the same black keys but in the middle to upper register.

To end the improvisation, the third pianist(s) should drop out, then the second, and finally the first.

COMPOSING PROJECT

Black-Key Piece

Create a piano piece using only the black keys.

Step 1. Using the five black keys, experiment playing a drone or an ostinato in one hand. This repetitive part should establish the steady rhythmic background for the melody.

Step 2. The other hand should explore any of the black keys. Experiment with many ideas until you decide on something that you like.

Step 3. If you wish to notate the pitches in your piece, write down the letter names of the notes. Lines can be used for shorter and longer durations.

Example:

RH   F#   F#   C#   D#

LH   C#

        F#

Step 4. With a classmate, take turns playing your pieces for each other. Assess your work for accuracy and creativity.

Indeterminacy

Indeterminacy refers to contemporary music in which the outcome or result is unpredictable. Contemporary composers give the performer(s) a framework within which to explore sounds, but no two performances using the framework are the same.

"Doodling" is an example of indeterminate music. Look up information about the composer in Biographical Sketches of *PianoLab* composers (Appendix M).

For "Doodling," follow the written directions of composer Tom Johnson. Before you begin, you could set up a tape recorder to record your piece. Later, play back and listen to your composition.

Doodling

Tom Johnson (United States, b. 1939)

Begin some very soft doodling with your right hand in the upper part of the keyboard. Continue the doodling as you read. Do not let your playing distract you from your reading, and do not let your reading distract you from your playing. The two must accompany each other. Now, without stopping the right-hand doodling, play a loud low note with your left hand, and sustain it for a moment. Continue the doodling and, whenever you feel the time is right, play another loud bass note. Do not wait too long between the loud low notes, but do not play them too close together either. Try not to worry about when you should or should not play another loud low note. If you become too involved with thinking about that, you will not be able to carry out your other tasks as well. Your attention should always be about equally divided between the three things: the reading, the right-hand doodling and the loud low notes.

Of course, you are quite limited in what you are permitted to play at the moment, and the music might become tedious after a while to someone who was only listening. But that is immaterial since these are *Private Pieces*, and are only for your own entertainment. The piece will not be tedious to you since it is not easy to do three things at once. The only way you can do all three well is by dividing your attention equally between them, so that you never ignore one of them. If you forget about the doodling, it will not sound the way you want it to sound. If you forget about the loud low notes, there will be a long awkward gap in the music. If you forget about the reading, you may miss some instruction or idea.

After another paragraph, you will be asked to play something else, but in the meantime continue playing and reading as you have been. If you find that you have been paying more attention to one of your tasks than to the other two, try to balance your attention more equally. Although no more instructions are necessary at the moment, the text is continuing in order to give you time to achieve a sense of balance between the three things, so that they seem to accompany one another. You have three more sentences in which to try to achieve this balance before going on to a new section of the piece. Now only two sentences, including this one, remain before the paragraph will end and you will be asked to do something else. This is the last sentence of this part of the piece.

Now stop playing, but continue reading. At some point during this paragraph, play a single note and sustain it. It may be loud or soft, high or low, black or white, but it must be a single note, and must be played only once. You may choose to play it early in the paragraph, or you may wish to play it toward the end of the paragraph. Perhaps you will want to read more of the text before making your decision. You must, however, remain within the limits of the paragraph. So if you have not played your note by this time, you must do so soon, as the paragraph is almost finished. You may wish to pause a moment before proceeding to the next paragraph, which will be quite demanding.

Resume the doodling with your right hand, as you did in the beginning of the piece, but this time let it gradually become more energetic. For a while it can be played by the right hand only, and should sound as it did at the beginning, but soon it should become faster. As it accelerates, you will probably want to use the left hand too, so that you can play more and more notes in less and less time. As the doodling becomes faster, you should also let it move into a wider range. By now the doodling should be noticeably more energetic than when you began this section. Do not let it increase too quickly, however, as there is still quite a ways to go before it reaches a peak. Gradually begin to use more and more of the keyboard and let the intensity increase until it is quite furious. Do not let the tension subside, even for a moment, and continue building until you are playing as wildly as you can. You may play anything necessary to maintain the high energy level. By now you should be playing as loud and fast as you can. You will perhaps find it more difficult to concentrate on the text now than when you were not playing so vigorously, but try to read the text as carefully as you have been, without making any sacrifices in your playing. Continue playing as wildly as you can, and look for ways that will enable you to play even more wildly. Do not be afraid to make booming or crashing sounds, if they will fit in with what you are already doing. When you find yourself running out of ideas or energy and want to end the piece, play one enormous crash and stop. Then listen for a moment to the silence.

CHAPTER EVALUATION

1. Demonstrate the correct hand, arm, and body positions for piano playing.

2. Play and name any pitch on black or white keys.

3. Improvise a simple black-key melody. Either alternate the hands or play a drone with one hand and the melody with the other.

4. Identify the designated keys on the following chart. Write below the keyboard for the white keys and above the keyboard for the black keys.

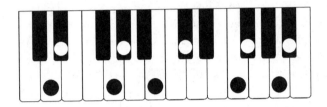

5. Describe the following musical terms:

   a. Flat

   b. Sharp

   c. Enharmonics

   d. Drone

   e. Ostinato

   f. Improvisation

   g. Indeterminacy

6. Identify the following musical symbols:

   a. ‖: :‖

   b. ♭

   c. ♯

2

Whole Steps and Half Steps
Major Five-Finger Pattern
Rhythm and Pitch Notation
Legato Touch
Parallel Motion
Independent Finger Action

WHOLE STEPS AND HALF STEPS

The distance from one pitch to another (*interval*) may be measured in whole steps and half steps. Pitches that are adjacent, or the shortest distance apart, are called **half steps** (for example, C to C♯, C♯ to D). There are two pairs of white keys that are naturally a half step apart—B to C and E to F.

Pitches that are adjacent are called half steps.

half steps

All adjacent keys on the keyboard are a half step apart. (The **chromatic scale,** a twelve-tone scale, proceeds entirely in half steps.) One fingering approach for playing up or down in half steps is to use finger 3 on black keys and fingers 1 and 2 on white keys (2 only on consecutive white keys). Notice that the LH fingering going down is the same as the RH going up and vice versa. Begin on any key and play up every black and white key.

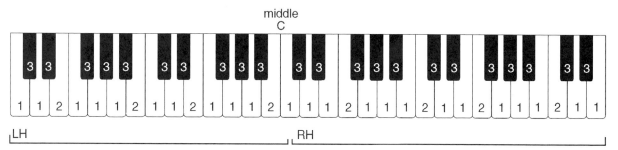

21

A **whole step** includes two half steps; for example, the interval from C to D is a whole step because it is made up of two half steps (C to C♯ and C♯ to D). Therefore, on the keyboard, one key (black or white) always comes between the pitches of a whole step. Begin on any key and play up in whole steps. Say the letter names, using sharps to identify black keys. Then find a new pitch and play down in whole steps. Say the letter names, using flats to name the black keys.

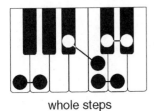

Whole steps include two half steps.

whole steps

MAJOR FIVE-FINGER PATTERN

The whole-step–half-step arrangement of the *major five-finger pattern* (the first five notes of a major scale) is as follows:

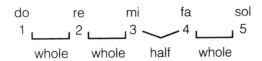

All five notes in the pattern are consecutive letter names. The first pitch of the pattern is called the *tonic* or *do*. Any key or pitch can be used as the tonic.

Playing the C Major Five-Finger Pattern

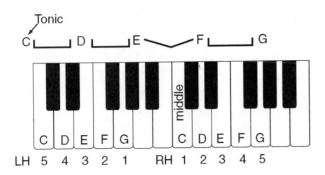

1. Play each key of the C major five-finger pattern, first up and then down. Say or sing the pitch names as you play.

2. Say the whole-step–half-step arrangement as you play the C major five-finger pattern: tonic, whole step, whole step, half step, whole step.

3. Play the C major five-finger pattern, calling out the correct finger numbers. Notice that in the RH, the tonic (bottom note or starting note) is played with the thumb (1), whereas in the LH, the tonic (bottom note or starting note) is played with the little finger (5).

4. Play the following exercise using the C major five-finger pattern. Play hands separately and hands together. Try playing in a smooth, connected manner.

Major Five-Finger Exercise

5. Play "The Rose" (from the 1979 musical film that starred Bette Midler) using the C major five-finger pattern. Practice hands separately and then hands together. A Piano 2 part for the instructor follows.

The Rose (from the film *The Rose*) (excerpt)

Piano 1 (Students)   Amanda McBroom (United States)

RH 1
C D | E (hold) E F E | E D D E D | C C D C | C
LH 5

C D | E E F E | E D D E D | C C D C | C

Piano 2 (Instructor)   Arranged by Dee Spencer

Andante

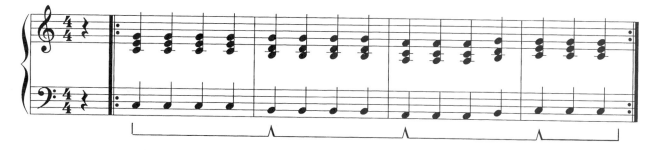

6. Play the familiar song "When the Saints Go Marching In" with the C major
five-finger pattern. A Piano 2 part for the instructor follows.

When the Saints Go Marching In*

Piano 1 (Students)   African-American Spiritual

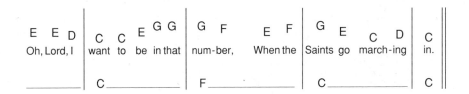

Piano 2 (Instructor)   Arranged by Eric Tamm

*Song notation is on page 72.

Playing Major Five-Finger Patterns

1. Spell and play the major five-finger patterns on the given tonic. Use a different letter name for each note. Remember to locate the tonic with the RH thumb and the LH little finger. Rest the other fingers on the four remaining pitches in the major pattern.

Major Five-Finger Pattern

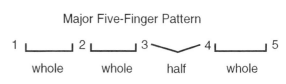

a. __C__ ____ ____ ____ ____

b. __D__ ____ ____ ____ ____

c. __E__ ____ ____ ____ ____

d. __F__ ____ ____ ____ ____

e. __G__ ____ ____ ____ ____

f. __A__ ____ ____ ____ ____

g. __B__ ____ ____ ____ ____

h. __C♯__ ____ ____ ____ ____

i. __E♭__ ____ ____ ____ ____

j. __F♯__ ____ ____ ____ ____

k. __A♭__ ____ ____ ____ ____

l. __B♭__ ____ ____ ____ ____

2. Practice the Major Five-Finger Exercise on p. 00 in different major five-finger patterns.

NOTES AND RESTS

Rhythm refers to all the **durations** of sounds and silences in music. **Notes** are the symbols used to represent durational sounds, and **rests** are used to indicate silences.

Note parts

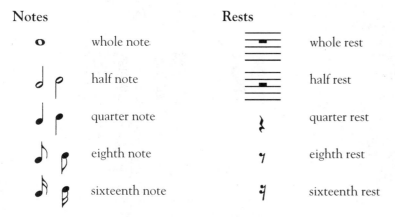

A notehead can be open (longer-duration notes) or solid (shorter-duration notes). The stems extend upward from the right or downward from the left of the notehead. Flags on both upward and downward stems always curl to the right.

Notes   **Rests**

o	whole note			whole rest
	half note			half rest
	quarter note			quarter rest
	eighth note			eighth rest
	sixteenth note			sixteenth rest

Beams

Notes with flags are frequently beamed together in groups.

Single flags take single beams: or

Multiple flags take multiple beams: or

Relative Note Durations

Notes are of relative duration, one to the other.

| 1 whole note equals |
| 2 half notes equal |
| 4 quarter notes equal |
| 8 eighth notes equal |
| 16 sixteenth notes |

BEAT AND METER

Most music has a steady **beat** or pulse. Beats are organized into groups, referred to as **meter.** Some beats are stressed more than others and become grouped in twos (**duple meter**), threes (**triple meter**), or fours (**quadruple meter**). The first beat in each meter is a strong beat or primary **accent** (´) and is followed by weaker, unaccented beats (ˇ). In quadruple meter, there is a secondary accent (–) on beat 3.

Meter

Duple Meter (2s):	1́	2̆		
Triple Meter (3s):	1́	2̆	3̆	
Quadruple Meter (4s):	1́	2̆	3̄	4̆

Meter Signatures

The two numbers, one above the other, that appear at the very beginning of a piece of music constitute the **meter signature** or **time signature.** The top number specifies the beat grouping, or meter, and the bottom number indicates the note that gets the beat.

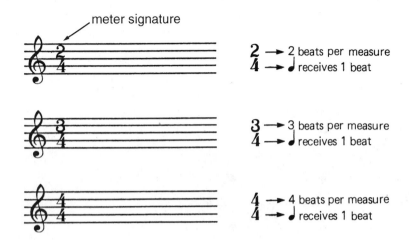

Frequently Used Meter Signatures (Simple Meter)

The following meters are referred to as **simple** because the beat in each divides into two equal parts.

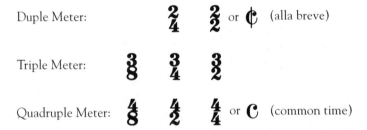

Duple Meter: **2/4** **2/2** or **₵** (alla breve)

Triple Meter: **3/8** **3/4** **3/2**

Quadruple Meter: **4/8** **4/2** **4/4** or **C** (common time)

Bar Lines

Vertical **bar lines** are used to indicate the meter or beat grouping and divide the music into **measures.** A double bar line is used at the end of a composition or section.

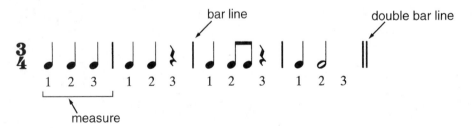

Rhythm Exercise 1: Duple and Quadruple Meters (○, ⌀, ♩, ♫) Clap, chant, or play the following rhythmic lines on any keys(s). The numbers under the notes refer to each consecutive beat in the measure (the top number of the meter signature), and these numbers are often spoken to aid in reading rhythms. (The numbers in parentheses are not clapped or played, but are counted.) Use the number counting system or any counting method recommended by your instructor.

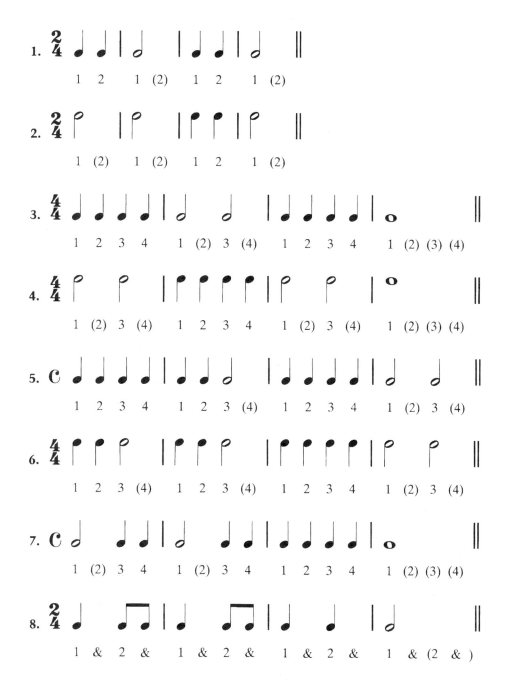

(continued)

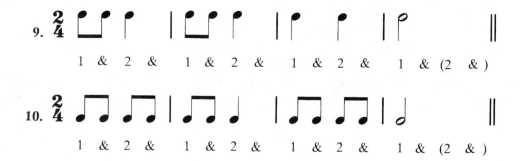

9. $\frac{2}{4}$

  1 & 2 &   1 & 2 &   1 &   2 &   1 & (2 &)

10. $\frac{2}{4}$

  1 & 2 &   1 & 2 &   1 & 2 &   1 & (2 &)

Performing Melodies

1. Determine the number of beats each note receives in "Aura Lee." Count the beats as you clap the rhythm. Play the melody using the C major five-finger pattern, hands separately.

Aura Lee*   American Folk Song

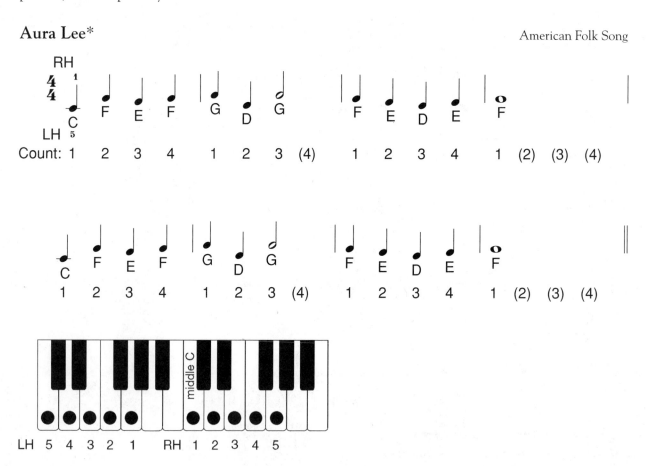

2. Determine the number of beats each note receives in "Chorale Melody." Clap and count the rhythm of the melody before playing it with the G major five-finger pattern, hands separately.

*Song notation is on page 275.

Chorale Melody*

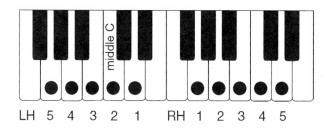

Rhythm Exercise 2: Two-Part Rhythms When playing the piano, one must perform two rhythms simultaneously—one with the RH and one with the LH. These examples should be performed by tapping or playing on any key the notes on the bottom line with one hand and the notes on the top line with the other hand. Perform each line separately, then hands together.

*A **chorale** is a hymn tune of the German Protestant church. Many compositions (especially in the seventeenth and eighteenth centuries) have been based on chorale melodies.

TREBLE AND BASS CLEF NOTATION

Pitches are notated on a staff, and two staves are often used in piano music.

 **Staff** Pitches are notated on a staff of five lines and four spaces.

 **Bass clef** or **F-clef** Clef that is written with a dot above and below the fourth line (F) of the lowest staff.

 **Grand** or **great staff** Two staves bracketed together, one with a treble clef and one with a bass clef. The upper staff is usually played by the RH, and the lower staff is usually played by the LH.

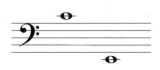 **Leger** (or **ledger**) **lines** Short lines added above or below the staff to extend the pitch range.

 **Treble clef** or **G-clef** Clef that encircles the second line (G) on the upper staff.

 **Stem** Vertical line attached to a notehead; stems go up on notes below the middle line and down on notes above the middle line of the staff.

The following grand staff includes the notation for white keys of the piano. When black keys are indicated, sharps and flats are placed before the note on the same line or space as the notehead or after the clef sign as a key signature on each staff of music. (See Appendix B for a grand staff with notation for both white and black keys.)

Grand staff

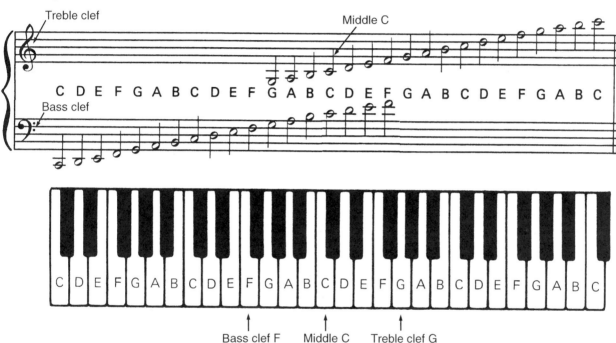

Pitch-Reading Exercise

1. Beginning with the lowest C on the bass clef staff above, play and name aloud the bass clef notes up to middle C (with your left hand), and then play the notes going back down.

2. Beginning with middle C on the treble clef staff, play and name the treble clef notes up to high C (with your right hand), and then reverse the naming and playing back to middle C. Memorize the names and their staff positions.

3. Sing the letter names and play the following musical examples in different major five-finger patterns. Look at the music, not at your hands, to develop confidence in your sense of touch.

C major

G major

D major

A major

4. Notate "Aura Lee" (p. 30) and "Chorale Melody" (p. 31) in treble and bass clef notation. Then play while reading from staff notation.

KEY SIGNATURES

The sharps (♯) or flats (♭) to be played throughout a piece are traditionally placed *after* the clef sign on each staff and *before* the meter signature. This grouping of sharps or flats is called a **key signature.** For example, if there is a sharp on the F line, all F's in the music should be performed as F-sharp rather than F-natural (♮). If a flat appears on the B line, all B's should be performed as B-flat rather than B-natural.

Key signature   Play all F's as F-sharp.   *Key signature*   Play all B's as B-flat.

Sometimes sharps or flats may appear in the key signature and not be used in the composition. In addition to specifying which notes will be sharped or flatted, the key signature identifies the **key** of the piece. Chapters 6 and 9 present information on major and minor key signatures.

Performing Melodies (Treble and Bass Clefs)

For each of the following melodies:

1. Count and clap the rhythm.
2. Place hand in the correct five-finger pattern.
3. "Finger" the melody without producing any sound.
4. Play, looking at the music, not at your hands.

Au Clair de la Lune

French Folk Melody

Folk Melody 1

Russian Folk Melody

Folk Melody 2

Folk Melody 3

Love Somebody   American Folk Song

John Lennon (England, 1940–1980)
Paul McCartney (England, b. 1942)

Help (excerpt)

*The first 3½ measures may be performed three times in succession.

†A **tie** (⌢) connects two identical notes. Play the first note only, and hold it through the time value of the second note.

Au Clair de la Lune

French Folk Melody

Folk Melody 1

Russian Folk Melody

Folk Melody 2

Folk Melody 3

Love Somebody

American Folk Song

John Lennon (England, 1940–1980)
Paul McCartney (England, b. 1942)

Help (excerpt)

COMPOSING PROJECT

Black-Key Melody

Create a melody using only the black keys.

> **Step 1.** As you play the following eight-measure rhythm, experiment with the five black keys. Try various pitches until you decide on something that you like.

> **Step 2.** Notate the letter names of the pitches in your melody above the rhythm (or on a staff). Use either all sharps or all flats; do not mix the two. Try a drone with your melody.

> **Step 3.** Play the melody, reading from the notation. Then, exchange your piece with a classmate's. Play your pieces for each other, and assess your work for accuracy and creativity.

ENSEMBLE PLAYING

Class-piano situations offer opportunities for two or more students to play together—sometimes all on the same part with the instructor performing something different, and sometimes with several pianists performing different parts. Performing with others requires playing exactly in time and listening carefully for good balance in the ensemble.

---

*The first 3½ measures may be performed three times in succession.

†A tie (‿) connects two identical notes. Play the first note only, and hold it through the time value of the second note.

Chapter 2 Ensemble Pieces:

1. "Recreation I" (Sartorio), pp. 278–279
2. "Recreation II" (Sartorio), pp. 280–281

REPERTOIRE

Visually analyze each of the following pieces, and determine the tonic, the major five-finger pattern, and the meter for each. Look up information about the composers in the *PianoLab* Composers section (Appendix M). (No information about Beyer has been located.) After learning each composer's birthdate and death date, determine the historical period (for example, Classic) in which each composer lived by referring to the Timeline of Western Art Music and History (Appendix K). Review the musical characteristics of the period. Look up **tempo** (*moderato*) and **dynamic** (f) terms in Appendix A.

"Unison Melody" and Etudes No. 12 and No. 13 should be performed **legato** (playing in a smooth, connected manner), often indicated by a curved line (**slur**) above or below the pitches. Review Technique Exercise 1 in this chapter. Then practice each piece hands separately and hands together. Notice that the two hands move in the same direction (**parallel motion**) for "Unison Melody" and independently in the two etudes.

Unison Melody (No. 1 from *First Term at the Piano*)

Moderato   Béla Bartók (Hungary, 1881–1945)

Etude No. 12

Moderato   Ferdinand Beyer (1803–1863)

Etude No. 13

Ferdinand Beyer (1803–1863)

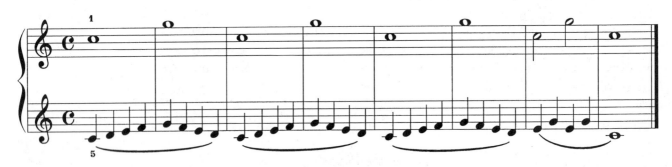

TECHNIQUE EXERCISES

Technical development is an important part of piano playing. In addition to studying and playing the musical examples in each chapter, you also need to practice specific exercises to increase your technical facility and tonal control. In fact, each time you sit down to play the piano, make it a habit to warm up with a technical exercise or two.

Before practicing any of these technique exercises, check your hand position at the keyboard.

Are your hands slightly arched?

Are your fingers gently curved? Is the fleshy part of your fingers striking the keys?

Are your fingernails short?

Are your wrists and arms straight but flexible?

Exercise 1: Legato Touch Legato touch requires playing in a smooth, connected manner. You must hold down each key, lifting as you play the next key without a break between them. The second key must go down as the first is coming up. Let the weight of your arms shift from one finger to the next while you keep a good hand position and a flexible wrist.

The following examples can be played with any major five-finger pattern, hands separately and hands together.

Part A

Part B

Part C

Exercise 2: Independent Finger Action Your fingers must become independent and strong. Practice this exercise very slowly. Begin with a good hand position. Make certain that the fingers strike the keys from a height of about half an inch without moving the top of the hand and wrist. Play legato (hold each key, lifting as you play the next key). Play the following patterns, beginning on any note.

Part A

Part B

CHAPTER EVALUATION

1. Demonstrate whole- and half-step distances at the keyboard.

2. Play a major five-finger pattern on the following tonics: C, G, D, A, and F.

3. Clap, chant, or play the rhythm of any melody or rhythm example in this chapter.

4. Demonstrate keyboard recognition of pitches notated in the treble and bass clefs.

5. Perform one of the melodies in this chapter with pitch and rhythmic accuracy and using correct fingering.

6. Demonstrate legato playing by performing an example from Technique Exercise 1 in this chapter.

7. Identify each interval as a half step or a whole step.

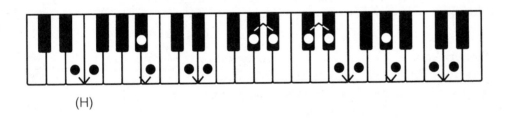

(H)

8. Identify the whole-step–half-step arrangement of the major five-finger pattern:

   1 (whole) 2 _____ 3 _____ 4 _____ 5

9. Identify the letter names for all the treble and bass clef pitches in the following example.

Sonata XXXIV (excerpt)   Domenico Scarlatti (Italy, 1685–1757)

10. Notate the following major five-finger patterns on the staff and keyboard chart. Circle the tonic pitch for each. When **accidentals** are needed, write the sharps or the flats on the staff *before* the pitches on the *same* line or in the *same* space.

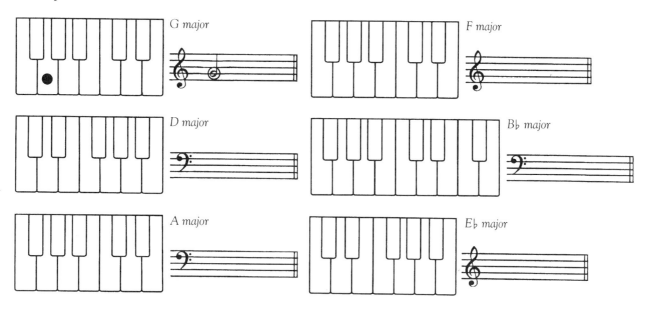

11. Write numbers under the notes to refer to each consecutive beat in the measure.

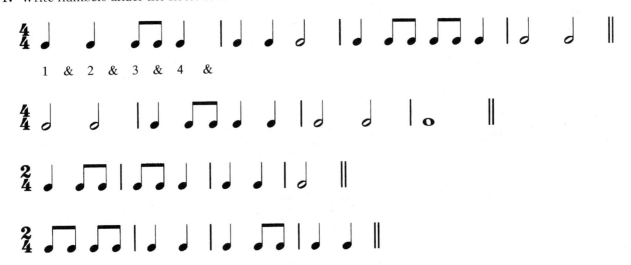

1   &   2   &   3   &   4   &

12. Create and notate four measures of rhythm for each of the following meter signatures.

13. Describe the following musical terms:

    a. Whole step   **b.** Half step

    c. Meter signature   **d.** Measure

    e. Duple meter   **f.** Legato touch

    g. Quadruple meter   **h.** Moderato

14. Identify the following musical symbols:

    a.   b.

    c.   d. o

    e.   f.

    g.   h. ***f***

INTERVAL READING

Learning to recognize musical distances is important in reading and performing music. In music, **interval** is the term used to describe the distance between two tones. First, you need to identify the intervals in music notation; then, you must develop a feel for the keyboard distances of those intervals. For example, when notes are on adjacent lines and spaces on the staff, you move from one key to the next (and from one letter name to the next) at the keyboard.

When notes skip from one space to the next space or from one line to the next line, you skip one piano key (and one letter name).

The following intervals are commonly used in major five-finger melodies. Any interval can be written or performed with the two pitches occurring successively (called a *melodic interval*) or with the two pitches sounding simultaneously (called a *harmonic interval*).

Intervals in the Major Five-Finger Pattern

Intervals are identified by *number* and *quality*. The number identification is determined by the number of letter names covered by the two notes. For example, C to E is called a third because there are three letter names (C, D, E) covered between the pitches.

Number Identification

C major

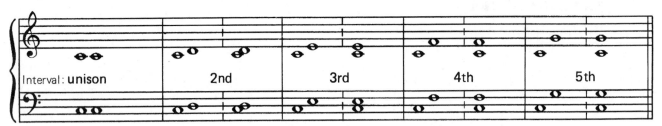

The quality of each interval is determined by the precise number of half steps between the two notes. In the major five-finger pattern, the qualities of the intervals formed with the tonic pitch are either major (M) or perfect (P). For example, C to E includes four half steps and is therefore classified as a major third (M3).

Number and Quality Identification

C major

perfect unison (P1)	major 2nd (M2)	major 3rd (M3)	perfect 4th (P4)	perfect 5th (P5)

Half steps: 0   2   4   5   7

Interval Exercises

1. Read and play each interval in the major five-finger pattern. Feel the distances, and listen to the sound of each interval.

2. Play these intervals in the following exercise. Practice one hand at a time.

Major Five-Finger Interval Exercise

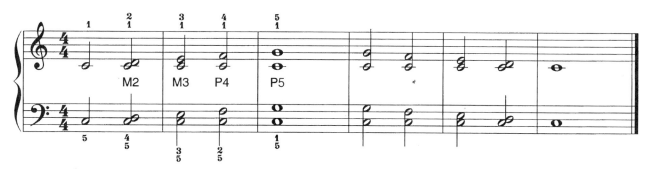

3. Identify the marked intervals by number and quality in the following musical excerpt.

One Moment in Time (excerpt)
(1988 Olympics, Seoul)

Words and music by
Albert Hammond and John Bettis

I want___   one mo-ment___   in   time   when I'm   more than___   I thought I ___could   be

4. Practice the intervals in the major five-finger pattern in Technique Exercise 3 in this chapter.

Performing Melodies—Interval Reading

As you perform the following melodies, first *look* at the notation and try to identify the interval distances between pitches by sight. Then try to *feel* the keyboard distances of those intervals as you play each piece. For additional interval reading, perform any of the pieces in Chapter 2, noticing interval distances.

Etude No. 14

Ferdinand Beyer (1803–1863)

Matarile

Folk Melody 4

TRANSPOSITION

Changing a melody from one key (scale) or five-finger pattern to another is called **transposition.** For example, if you play "When the Saints Go Marching In" in the C major pattern and then play it in the G major pattern, you have transposed the song from the key of C to the key of G. Because all the intervals are parallel, the two versions should sound exactly the same—only higher or lower.

There are several approaches to transposition. One is to identify each pitch in the piece to be transposed by its number position in the scale or pattern. Then change each number to the letter name of the new scale or pattern. For example, in "The Old Oak Tree" the major five-finger pattern is G and the numbers for each note are: G = 1, A = 2, B = 3, C = 4, D = 5. In the transposed version, the F major five-finger pattern is used and the numbers are: F = 1, G = 2, A = 3, B♭ = 4, C = 5. Note how the two versions use the same pitch number.

The Old Oak Tree

G major (original)   English Folk Melody

F major (transposed)

A major (transposed)

Another way to transpose is to calculate the interval distances between the pitches in the piece to be transposed and then use those same interval distances for the new version. For example, when "The Old Oak Tree" is transposed from G major to F major, it requires shifting every pitch down a major second, or a whole step.

Transposition Practice

1. Perform the two versions of "The Old Oak Tree" above. Feel the similarity in keyboard distances.

2. On the blank staff provided after "The Old Oak Tree" (p. 49), notate a transposition of this melody. Transpose to the A major five-finger pattern. Use either of the transposition approaches described above. Play your transposition and check for accuracy.

3. At the keyboard, transpose some or all of the following pieces (or any in Chapters 2 and 3).

> Folk Melody 1, p. 35, to G major
>
> Russian Folk Melody, p. 37, to C major
>
> Unison Melody, p. 39, to D major
>
> Etude No. 12, p. 40, to G major
>
> Matarile, p. 48, to F major
>
> Folk Melody 4, p. 48, to C major

Guidelines for Transposition

Approach 1: Scale Position

Step 1. Determine the scale or five-finger pattern of the piece to be transposed. Identify each pitch in the piece by its number in the five-finger pattern or scale.

Step 2. Decide what scale or five-finger pattern you will use for the transposed version. Number each pitch. Then, change each pitch number in the original piece to the letter name of the pitch in the new scale or five-finger pattern.

Approach 2: Intervals

Step 1. Determine the scale or five-finger pattern of the piece to be transposed. Decide what scale or five-finger pattern you will use for the transposed version.

Step 2. Calculate the interval distances between the pitches in the original scale or five-finger pattern and in the pattern to which it will be transposed (e.g., G major to F major results in shifting every pitch down a M2, or a whole step). Then, change each pitch to the correct pitch in the new scale or five-finger pattern.

RHYTHM

Rhythm Exercise 1: Duple and Quadruple Meters (o, ∂, ∂, $\partial\partial$, ξ, $-$) Clap, chant, or play the following rhythmic lines on any key(s). Use the number counting system or any counting method recommended by your instructor.

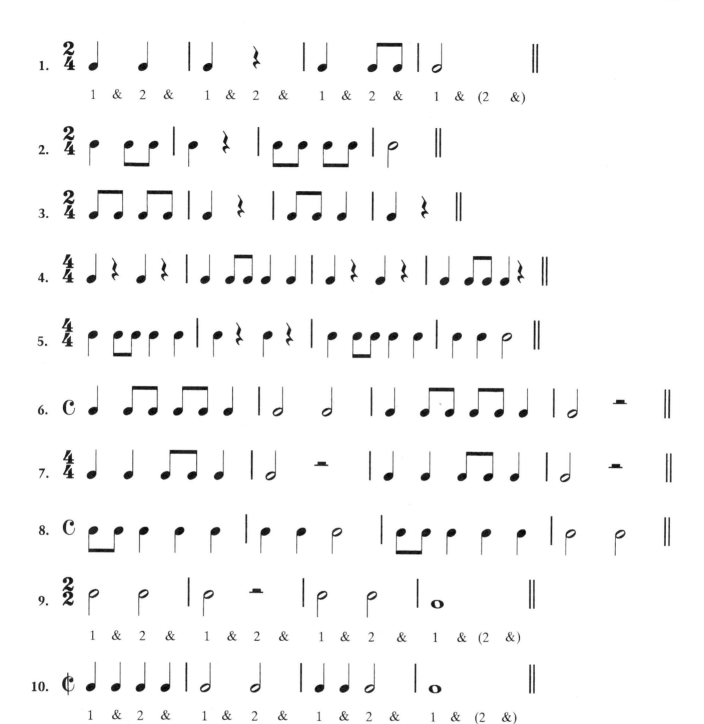

Rhythm Exercise 2: Two-Part Rhythms Perform by tapping or playing on any key(s) the notes on the bottom line with one hand and the notes on the top line with the other hand. Perform each line hands separately and then hands together.

HARMONY

CHORDS

The building blocks of harmony are **chords.** *A chord consists of three or more pitches a third apart, sounded simultaneously.* Chords are often played with the left hand to provide an accompaniment for a melody.

Since playing three or more notes simultaneously may be a challenge to beginning pianists, chord accompaniments can be simplified by playing only one tone of the chord. Of the chord tones, the **chord root** (bottom note) is the strongest.

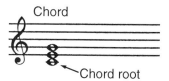

Chord Symbols

In jazz and in popular and folk music, the names of chord roots are used in a symbol system called *lead sheet notation.* Uppercase letters are written above the staff, specifying what chords should be used and when they should be played. The single pitch indicated by the chord symbol is the chord root. (When a number appears next to a capital letter, a four-note chord is indicated.)

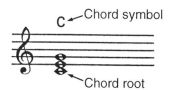

To add a chord-root accompaniment to a melody, play with your left hand the single pitch indicated by the chord symbol. Play the roots an octave lower than the melody and on the strong beats of the measure. Play the same chord root until a new symbol is given.

Kris Kristofferson (United States, b. 1936)
Fred Foster

Me and Bobby McGee (excerpt)

Performing Melodies with Chord-Root Accompaniment

Guidelines for Performing Chord-Root Accompaniments

Step 1. Locate the chord symbols for each melody. Notice that in the following melodies the chord roots for each are the first (I) and fifth (V) tones of the major five-finger pattern. Remember that the I is called the *tonic* and the V is called the *dominant*.

Step 2. When playing the chord roots in the LH, you may use the little finger for the tonic (I) and the thumb for the dominant (V). Or you may play the tonic (I) with your thumb and the dominant (V) *below* the tonic by using your little finger. Try both the *dominant above* and the *dominant below* positions and decide which sounds better for each melody.

Step 3. When playing the chord roots in the RH, use the thumb for the tonic (I) and the little finger for the dominant (V).

Step 4. Play a chord root on beat 1 in each measure.

Little River

German Folk Melody

Jim-Along Josie

American Folk Melody

English Folk Melody 1

Chilean Folk Melody

At the keyboard, transpose one or two of the preceding folk melodies ("Little River," "Jim-Along Josie," English, and Chilean) to other major patterns. To transpose the chord-root accompaniment, remember that the chord roots will be the first and fifth pitches of the major pattern.

Performing Chord Roots from Staff Notation

1. Chord roots for the following melodies are written out in the bass and treble clefs. Strive for a good balance between hands. Transpose to other major patterns.

Hungarian Folk Melody 1

Danish Folk Melody

American Folk Melody 1

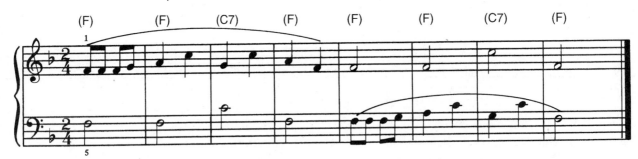

2. Write out the chord-root accompaniment in staff notation for "Little River," p. 54; "Jim-Along Josie," p. 54; English Folk Melody 1, p. 54; and Chilean Folk Melody, p. 55.

COMPOSING PROJECT

Major Five-Finger Melody

Create a melody based on a selected major five-finger pattern.

Step 1. Choose a major five-finger pattern that you can play comfortably.

Step 2. Experiment with those five pitches as you perform the following eight-measure rhythm. Try various pitches until you decide on something that you like. Be sure to conclude your melody on the tonic.

Step 3. Notate your melody on the staff below, and then play, reading from staff notation. Exchange your melody with a classmate's. Play your pieces for each other, and assess your work for accuracy and creativity.

ENSEMBLE PLAYING

Chapter 3 Ensemble Pieces:

1. "Love Somebody," pp. 282–283
2. "J'ai du bon Tabac," pp. 282–283

REPERTOIRE

Visually analyze each of the following pieces, determining the tonic, the major five-finger pattern, and the meter for each. Look up information about the composers in the Biographical Sketches of *PianoLab* Composers (Appendix M). Then determine the historical period for each by reviewing the Timeline of Western Art Music and History (Appendix K). Check the meaning of op. (**opus**) in the Glossary and of *allegretto, moderato,* **p,** and **_mf_** in Appendix A.

In Op. 117, No. 5, both the RH and the LH parts are notated in the treble clef. Make sure that you place your hands in the correct location on the keyboard.

Op. 117, No. 5

Allegretto   Cornelius Gurlitt (Germany, 1820–1901)

Op. 218 includes imitation. Notice how the LH echoes the RH part in much of the piece. Both the RH and the LH parts stay within the C major five-finger pattern.

Op. 218

Moderato   Louis Köhler (Germany, 1820–1886)

TECHNIQUE EXERCISES

Before playing any of these exercises, check your hand position. Make sure you are comfortably seated at the piano.

Exercise 1: Contrary Motion Pianists must learn to coordinate their two hands playing together. When two hands move in opposite directions, the motion is called **contrary.**

Practice the following contrary-motion exercise, keeping the wrists flexible and the arms moving in a gentle outward and upward movement for each two-measure pattern in Part A. In Part B, the movements will be reversed. Transpose this exercise to the major five-finger patterns of G, D, A, E, F, and B.

Part A

Part B

Exercise 2: Independent Hands and Hand Coordination This exercise should be practiced in two parts. The first (Part A) focuses on the RH moving in quarter notes while the LH moves in whole notes. Part B reverses this rhythmic movement. Transpose to other major patterns.

Part A

Part B

Exercise 3: Intervals (Major Five-Finger Pattern) Play these intervals in the following pattern. Stress independent finger action, and work for a legato sound.

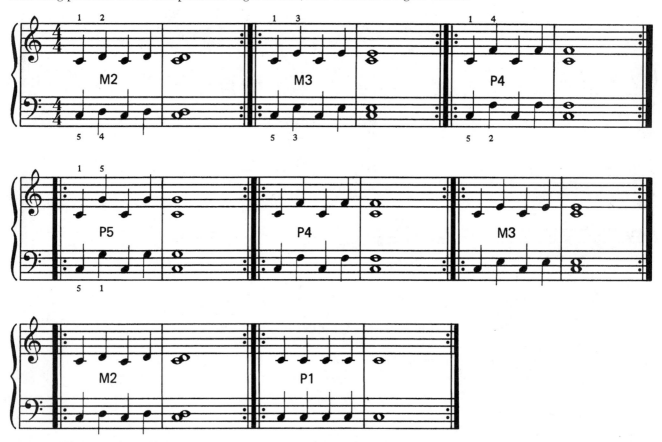

Exercise 4: Register Change Try to move as smoothly as possible as you change from one register to another. First play the five-finger pattern up the keyboard in C, and then play the five-finger pattern down the keyboard. Then transpose to other major patterns.

Part A

Part B

CHAPTER EVALUATION

1. Demonstrate intervals of perfect unisons, major seconds, major thirds, perfect fourths, and perfect fifths at the keyboard.

2. At the keyboard, transpose Folk Melody 2, on p. 36, from the F major five-finger pattern to the G major pattern.

3. Perform a chord-root accompaniment for Chilean Folk Melody, p. 55.

4. Demonstrate hand coordination in *contrary motion* by performing Technique Exercise 1 in this chapter.

5. Label the following intervals by quality and number, such as P5. Using the keyboard chart, count the number of half steps between the two notes. Remember: P1 = 0, M2 = 2, M3 = 4, P4 = 5. P5 = 7.

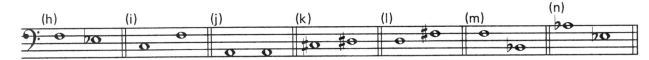

6. Complete the specified intervals by notating the second pitch above (↑) or
below (↓) the given pitch (as in melodic intervals). Use the keyboard chart
above to count the needed half steps for each.

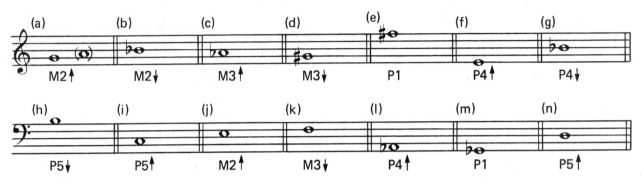

7. Transpose Op. 117, No. 5, on p. 57, to the D major five-finger pattern. Notate
the transposition. When accidentals are needed, write the sharps or the flats
on the staff *before* the notes on the *same* line or in the *same* space.

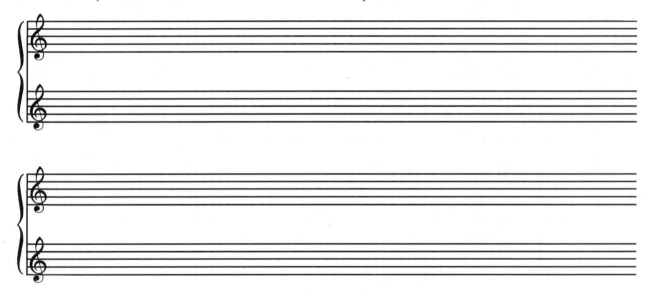

8. Notate the chord roots (in the bass clef) for each chord in the excerpt from
"Leavin' on a Jet Plane."

Leavin' on a Jet Plane (excerpt)   John Denver (United States, b. 1943)

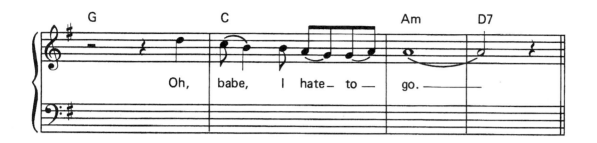

9. Describe the following musical terms:

    a. Interval

    b. Transposition

    c. Chord

    d. Chord root

    e. Lead sheet notation

10. Identify the following musical symbols:

    a. P1

    b. *mf*

    c. 𝄽

    d. ▬

    e. M2

    f. M3

    g. P5

    h. P4

4

Dotted Notes and Rests

Upbeats

Major Triad

Tonic Chord

Parallel and Contrasting Phrases

Memorizing

Expanded Hand Position

Hand-Position Shift

RHYTHM

DOTTED NOTES AND RESTS

Dots placed to the right of noteheads and rests give the notes and rests within a measure a longer duration. One dot increases the duration of the note or rest by one half. For example, a dotted half note is equal to the duration of three quarter notes.

♩. = ♩♩♩

Duet Exercise 32* (excerpt)

Andante   Ferdinand Beyer (1803–1863)

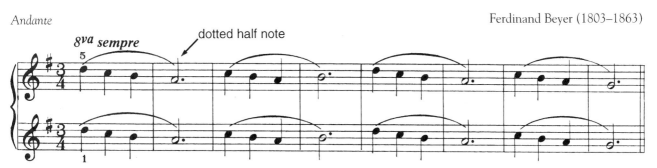

*The complete Duet Exercise 32 is on page 285.

Dotted Notes

$\boldsymbol{o}\cdot$ dotted whole note

$\boldsymbol{d}\cdot$ $\boldsymbol{\rho}\cdot$ dotted half note

$\boldsymbol{d}\cdot$ $\boldsymbol{\rho}\cdot$ dotted quarter note

$\boldsymbol{\jmath}\cdot$ $\boldsymbol{\rho}\cdot$ dotted eighth note

$\boldsymbol{\jmath}\cdot$ $\boldsymbol{\rho}\cdot$ dotted sixteenth note

Dotted Rests

dotted whole rest

dotted half rest

$\boldsymbol{\xi}\cdot$ dotted quarter rest

$\boldsymbol{\gamma}\cdot$ dotted eighth rest

$\boldsymbol{\gamma}\cdot$ dotted sixteenth rest

Rhythm Exercise 1: Dotted Notes Clap, chant, or play the following rhythmic lines on any key(s). Determine the number of counts each dotted note receives.

Performing Melodies with Dotted Notes

Visually analyze each melody; then count and clap the rhythm of each. Determine the number of beats each dotted note receives, and mark the beats for each measure. Transpose each melody to another major pattern.

Ode to Joy (from the fourth Movement, Symphony No. 9, Op. 125)

Ludwig van Beethoven (Germany, 1770–1827)

La Bamba (excerpt)

Mexican Wedding Song
Arranged by Ritchie Valens (United States, 1941–1959)

Largo Theme (from the *New World* Symphony)

Antonin Dvořák (Bohemia, 1841–1904)

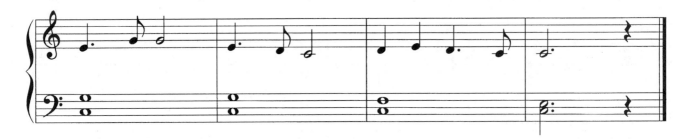

English Folk Melody 2

UPBEATS

The notes in the incomplete measure found at the beginning of many pieces are called the **upbeat** or the **anacrusis.** Often in short melodies, the upbeat (or "pickup" notes) and an incomplete last measure combine to make one complete measure. The notes in the upbeat are unaccented and actually anticipate the accent of the first beat in the first full measure.

Happy Birthday (excerpt)   Mildred and Patty Hill

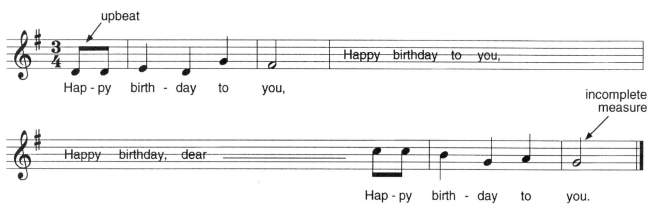

Rhythm Exercise 2: Upbeat, Triple Meter Clap, chant, or play the following rhythmic lines on any key(s). To perform the rhythmic lines that include an upbeat, count a full measure of beats first; then count the beat that precedes the upbeat. Be sure you know on which beat the upbeat falls.

Rhythm Exercise 3: Coordinated Rhythms (2 hands) Analyze, then perform these examples by tapping or playing on any key the notes on the bottom line with your LH and the notes on the top line with your RH. Perform each line separately and then perform the lines together.

Performing Melodies with Upbeats

For the following pieces, determine on which beat the upbeat falls. Count a full
measure of beats first; then count the beat or beats that precede the upbeat. Transpose each piece to another major pattern.

Minuet 10 (excerpt)   Franz Joseph Haydn (Austria, 1732–1809)

Standin' in the Need of Prayer   African-American Spiritual

When the Saints Go Marching In

African-American Spiritual

German Folk Melody 1

*A tie (⌢) connects two identical notes. Play the first note only, and hold it through the time value of the second note.

HARMONY

TRIADS

The most common chords are built by arranging intervals of thirds one above the other. The most basic chord of tonal music is the **triad,** a chord with three pitches. The three pitches of any triad are identified by the terms *root, third,* and *fifth.* The pitches can be performed with the root on the bottom (called *root position*) or may be rearranged into *inversions.* The root also gives the triad its name: C, F, and so on.

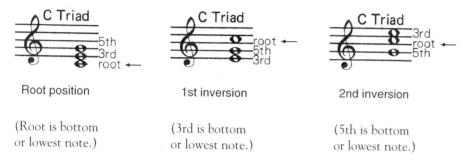

Root position

1st inversion

2nd inversion

(Root is bottom or lowest note.)

(3rd is bottom or lowest note.)

(5th is bottom or lowest note.)

Major Triad

By combining the *first, third,* and *fifth* pitches of the major five-finger pattern, one forms a **major triad.** The major triad always includes a *major third* (four half steps) between the root and the third, a *minor third* (three half steps) between the third and the fifth, and a *perfect fifth* (seven half steps) between the root and the fifth.

F major

G major

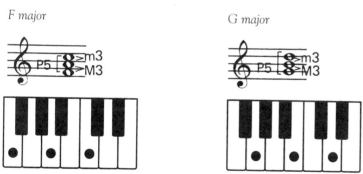

Performing Major Triads in Block-Chord Form

Practice the major triad in *block-chord form* (chord tones played simultaneously) in the following positions at the keyboard. Sit centered at the keyboard and far enough back to allow freedom of movement. To play the chords, push keys down simultaneously, with equal weight on each key. Try to connect playings of the chord as smoothly as possible. Be careful not to overlap the chords when hands cross. Transpose to G, F, D, A, and E.

Block-Chord Exercise: Major Triad

Part A

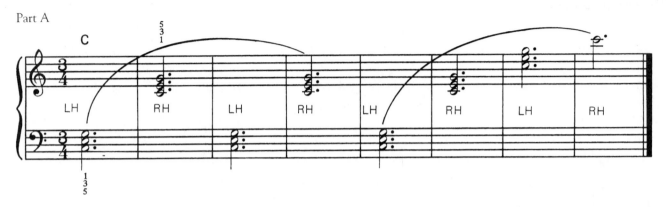

Part B

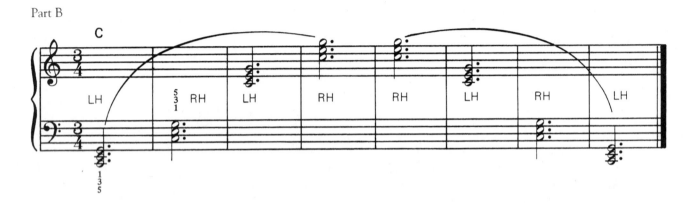

Performing Major Triads in Arpeggio Form

These exercises use the major triad in *broken-chord*, or **arpeggio,** *form* (chord tones played one after the other). Again, connect chord tones as smoothly as you can and use the hand-over-hand technique when specified. Hold the chord shape in the hand and touch each new key's location just before playing. Transpose to the major triads of F, G; D, A, E; and D♭, A♭, E♭. Learn the feel of these chords grouped by color of keys.

Arpeggio Exercise: Major Triad

Part A

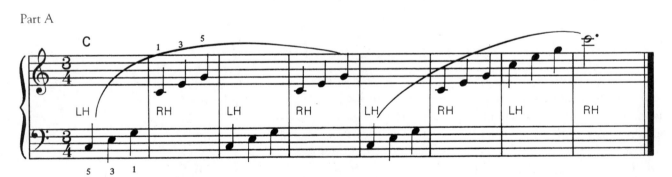

Part B

TONIC CHORD (MAJOR)

The first pitch of the major five-finger pattern is called the **tonic,** and the chord built on the first step is called the *tonic chord* or the I chord. The tonic chord for the major pattern is a major triad.

C major five-finger pattern —Tonic chord

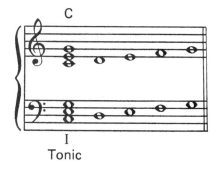

Tonic

Tonic Chord and Major Five-Finger Pattern

Locate the major triad built on the tonic for each major five-finger pattern. Play the following example in these major five-finger patterns: C, G, F; D, A, E; and D♭, A♭, E♭.

C major

Performing Melodies with Tonic Chord Accompaniments

The first three melodies are accompanied with the tonic chord of the major pattern. Perform with a good balance of sound between the melody and the chord (melody should dominate). Transpose to other major patterns.

Whistle Daughter

American Folk Song

Dressed in Blue

American Folk Song

Umptum Lady

American Folk Song

The next three melodies have the tonic chord as part of their accompaniment.
Observe the dynamic markings of *forte* (loud) and *piano* (soft).

Little River

German Folk Melody

American Folk Melody 2

Folk Melody 5

FORM

PHRASES

The overall design, plan, or order of a musical composition is referred to as its *form*. Most of the melodies studied so far are of a simple folk-song design. Even though the melodies are only eight to twelve measures long, they divide into smaller musical ideas known as **phrases.** In many of these melodies, the phrases (musical clauses or sentences) span approximately four measures. Pianists often punctuate the end of a phrase by a momentary lift or "breath."

Parallel Phrases

When two phrases begin with the same pitches and include almost identical material, the paired phrases are said to be *parallel*.

Israeli Folk Melody 1 illustrates parallel phrases (phrase 2 is almost identical to phrase 1). As you perform this melody with chord roots, be sure to lift slightly at the ends of the phrases. Notice that once you have learned the first phrase, you have almost learned the entire melody.

Israeli Folk Melody 1

Contrasting Phrases

When a second phrase (especially its beginning) includes musical materials that are different from those of the first phrase, the phrases are *contrasting*. Often one feels a question-and-answer type dialogue in paired contrasting phrases.

Folk Melody 6 is an example of contrasting phrases. Perform this melody with chord roots, marking the ends of phrases with a slight lift.

Folk Melody 6

Identify parallel or contrasting phrases in the following pieces:

German Folk Melody 1 (p. 72) _____

Minuet 10 (excerpt) by Haydn (p. 71) _____

Russian Folk Melody (p. 36) _____

"Ode to Joy" by Beethoven (p. 67) _____

"Allegro" by Türk (p. 82) _____

COMPOSING PROJECT

Parallel- and Contrasting-Phrase Melodies

Compose two melodies, one illustrating parallel phrases and one illustrating contrasting phrases. The first phrase for each melody is provided; write a second phrase of the same length. Use the F major five-finger pattern, and make sure you conclude on the tonic F.

> **Guidelines for Composing a Parallel Phrase**
>
> **Step 1.** For the first two measures of your second phrase (measures 5–6), notate the exact pitches used for the beginning of phrase 1 (measures 1–2).
>
> **Step 2.** For measures 7–8, be creative. Use the same pitches of the five-finger pattern, but in a different combination or rhythm from what was used for the concluding measures (3–4) of phrase 1. Be sure to end on the tonic pitch.
>
> **Step 3.** Play both phrases. Check to see that they look and sound parallel (the two begin the same and include almost identical pitches and rhythm; they are the same length). Exchange your notated melody with another student. Play your melodies for each other, and assess your work for accuracy and creativity.

Parallel-Phrase Melody

Melody 1—Parallel phrases

↑ tonic

Guidelines for Composing a Contrasting Phrase

Step 1. Play phrase 1 and be attentive to the exact pitches and rhythm.

Step 2. To create a contrasting phrase to pair with the first phrase, use the same pitches of the five-finger pattern but in a different combination. Experiment until you compose a phrase that is *contrasting* to phrase 1, but not so different that it does not seem to pair well enough to make a complete melody. (Using similar rhythmic patterns in the two phrases helps to unify the entire melody!) Be sure to conclude on the tonic.

Step 3. Play both phrases. Check to see that they look and sound contrasting (the two phrases begin and end with different pitches; they are the same length). Exchange your notated melody with another student's. Play your melodies for each other, and assess your work for accuracy and creativity.

Contrasting-Phrase Melody

Melody 2—Contrasting phrases

↑ tonic

ENSEMBLE PLAYING

Chapter 4 Ensemble Pieces:

1. Duet Exercise 32, pp. 284–285
2. Waltz, pp. 286–287

REPERTOIRE

Visually analyze the repertoire pieces, and determine the tonic, the finger position, the meter, and the phrase structure for each. Locate information about the composers in the Biographical Sketches of *PianoLab* Composers (Appendix M). Refer to the Timeline of Western Art Music and History (Appendix K) to place the composers in a historical period. Check the meaning of dynamic marking ***mf*** in Appendix A. Memorize one of the pieces.

Memorizing

Memorizing music requires several different kinds of skills. It is not enough to keep repeating a piece until your fingers can play it automatically. Your mind needs to guide your fingers for a lasting memorization.

First, a thorough understanding of the melody, rhythm, harmony, and form is necessary for recalling the total "picture" of the piece under study. This is achieved through analysis. Second, after you have performed a piece many times and studied the technical aspects, your fingers should know the physical movements. Third, you must be able to remember aurally the pitches and their rhythmic values.

Guidelines for Memorizing Pieces

Step 1. You are ready to memorize when you can play a piece with pitch and rhythmic accuracy and correct fingering (hands separately and hands together). In addition, you should have a sound knowledge of the characteristics of melody, rhythm, and form.

Step 2. Next, work on aurally recalling the pitches and the rhythm. Begin by dividing the piece into smaller parts. (In short compositions, these parts would be phrases.) Learn to play these smaller parts from memory with each hand separately. When you can do this easily, try playing each hand alone but using just one finger (index). This is a good test to see if you know the notes aurally without the aid of physical involvement.

Step 3. Play the smaller parts hands together from memory. Try playing with your eyes closed.

Step 4. Combine the smaller parts until the whole piece is memorized. Then try playing the piece with your eyes closed.

In the Kabalevsky piece, both the LH and the RH parts are notated in the treble clef. (The LH part extends beyond the five-finger pattern.) The short horizontal line above or below a note ($\bar{\rho}$) indicates that the note should be performed with a slight stress and that the tone should be sustained. Observe the phrasing, and work for a legato touch.

Melody, Op. 39, No. 1 (from *24 Little Pieces*)

Moderato   Dmitri Kabalevsky (Russia, 1904–1987)

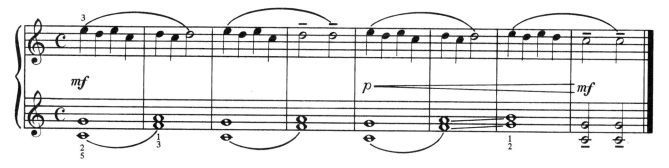

In "Allegro," the RH stays within the C major five-finger pattern (an octave above middle C). The LH, however, covers the range of an octave. Practice the LH fingering and range before playing the piece with hands together.

Allegro   Daniel Gottlob Türk (Germany, 1750–1813)

In "3 White-Note Clusters," a twentieth-century composition, the white and black rectangles are tone clusters of three notes. (Clusters are bunched seconds played simultaneously. Pitches in the cluster are determined by the position on the staff.) Play the *blocked clusters* with fingers 2, 3, and 4 in each hand.

Blocked clusters

3 White-Note Clusters (IV from *32 Piano Games*)

♩ = 80   Ross Lee Finney (United States, b. 1906)

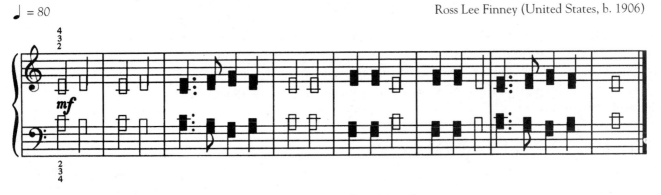

TECHNIQUE EXERCISES

Play all the exercises in the major patterns of C, G, D, A, F, E, and B.

Exercise 1: Independent Hands and Hand Coordination Review Exercise 2 on page 59 before playing this one. This exercise, like the one on page 00, is in two parts. Part A features the RH rhythmically moving in shorter durations against the longer durations of the LH. Part B reverses this rhythmic movement. Practice hands together and with each hand separately. Play legato, allowing only one note to sound at a time. Let the weight of your arm shift from one finger to the next while you keep a good hand position and a flexible wrist.

Part A

Part B

Exercise 2: Hand-Position Shift In this Bartók study, you will shift from the G major five-finger pattern to the D major pattern and then return to the G pattern. Practice this hand-position shift, trying not to look down at the keys.

Study: Changing Hand Position (from *First Term at the Piano*)

Moderato

Béla Bartók (Hungary, 1881–1945)

(continued)

CHAPTER EVALUATION

1. Perform with rhythmic accuracy the following pieces, which include anacrusis, dotted notes, or both: Minuet 10 (excerpt) by Haydn, p. 71, and English Folk Melody 2, p. 68.

2. Play major triads constructed on the tonic of the following major five-finger patterns: C, D, E♭, F, A, B♭. Perform in block-chord and broken-chord forms.

3. Transpose any melody in this chapter to another major five-finger pattern.

4. Perform by memory one of the pieces in this chapter.

5. Demonstrate hand-position shift by performing the "Study: Changing Hand Position" by Bartók, on p. 83.

6. Circle the upbeat in the following example. Indicate on what beat the upbeat begins.

The Star-Spangled Banner (excerpt)

John Stafford Smith (England, 1750–1836)
Francis Scott Key (United States, 1779–1843)

O_____ say! Can you see, by the dawn's ear - ly light,

7. For each dotted note, write the equivalent notes.

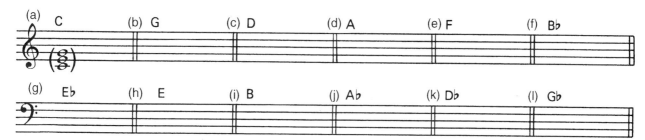

8. Write the designated major triads. When accidentals are needed, write the sharps or the flats on the staff *before* the notes.

(a) C   (b) G   (c) D   (d) A   (e) F   (f) B♭

(g) E♭   (h) E   (i) B   (j) A♭   (k) D♭   (l) G♭

9. Notate the A major five-finger pattern in the treble and bass clefs and the tonic (I) chord on the staff at right.

10. Describe the following musical terms:

    a. Phrase

    b. Parallel phrases

    c. Contrasting phrases

    d. Tonic chord

    e. Triad

    f. Major triad

    g. Upbeat

11. Identify the following musical symbols:

    a. 𝅗𝅥.

    b. 𝅘𝅥.

    c. *f*

    d. *p*

    e. ♮

5

Minor Five-Finger Pattern

Minor Triad

Extension Fingering

MINOR FIVE-FINGER PATTERN

The whole-step–half-step arrangement of the *minor five-finger pattern* (the first five notes of a minor scale) is as follows:

1 └─── 2 ⌄ 3 └─── 4 └─── 5
whole   half   whole   whole

A minor five-finger pattern, like the major one, can be built on any of the twelve keys or pitches. The whole-step–half-step pattern is illustrated on the white keys from A to E.

Playing the Minor Five-Finger Pattern

1. Notate the pitches for the following minor patterns. Follow the whole-half-whole-whole pattern exactly. Play each.

87

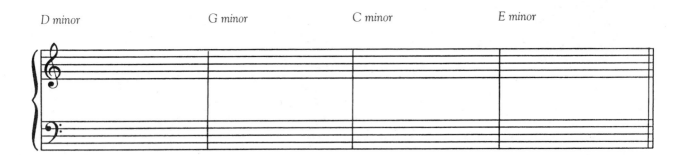

D minor   *G minor*   *C minor*   *E minor*

2. Play the following minor five-finger pattern exercise, moving as smoothly as possible from one register to another. First, play the pattern up the keyboard; then play down the keyboard. Transpose to other minor patterns.

Minor Five-Finger Register Exercise

Comparing Major and Minor Five-Finger Patterns

In the minor pattern, the third pitch is the only one that is different from the major pattern. To make a major five-finger pattern minor, lower the third tone a half step.

C major   *C minor*

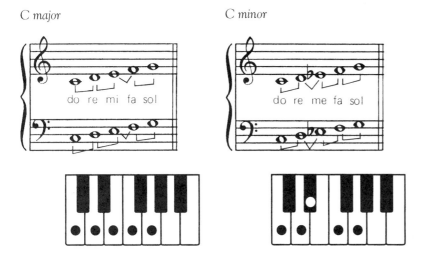

Playing Major and Minor Patterns

To hear and understand the contrast between the major and minor patterns, play the following exercise. Transpose the exercise to the five-finger patterns of G, D, A, F, E, and B.

C major / C minor

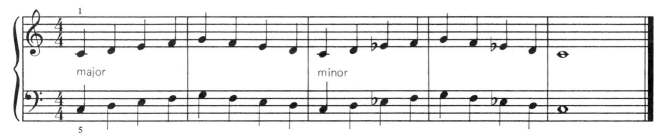

INTERVALS

In the minor five-finger pattern, the interval of the third is the only one that is different from the major pattern. The *minor third* is a half step smaller than the major third.

Intervals in the Minor Five-Finger Pattern

C minor

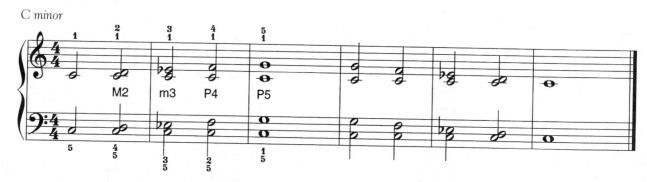

Interval Exercises

1. Read and play each interval in the minor five-finger pattern. Feel the distances and listen to the sound of each interval.

2. Play these intervals in the following exercise. Practice hands separately and hands together. Transpose to other minor five-finger patterns.

Minor Five-Finger Interval Exercise

C minor

3. Practice intervals in the minor five-finger pattern in Technique Exercise 2 and major and minor thirds in Technique Exercise 3 in this chapter.

4. Identify the marked intervals by number and quality in the following excerpt.

Riders on the Storm (excerpt)

Jim Morrison (United States, 1943–1971)

Ri - ders on the storm,   ri - ders on the storm,   in - to this house we're born,

Performing Minor Five-Finger Melodies

Sight-read the following minor melodies after visually analyzing each. Determine the minor pattern by checking the last note of the melody. Play the pattern in ascending and descending form. Check the meter, and clap and count the rhythm of the melody. Keep your eyes on the music, not on your hands. Feel the interval relationships between notes. Transpose to other minor patterns.

Middle Eastern Folk Melody

Czech Folk Melody 1

Moderato

Adagio

Daniel Gottlob Türk (Germany, 1750–1813)

German Folk Melody 2

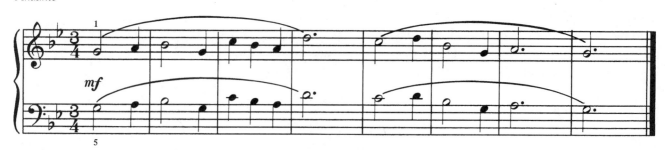

Erie Canal (excerpt)

HARMONY

MAJOR AND MINOR TRIADS

The only pitch that is different in parallel major and minor triads is the middle one. To change a major triad to a minor triad, lower the middle pitch a half step. In lead sheet notation, a capital letter followed by a lowercase *m* indicates a minor chord.

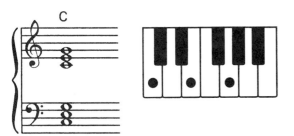

C major triad

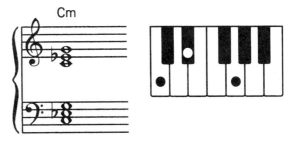

C minor triad

Performing Major and Minor Triads

1. Perform the following major and minor triad exercise. Feel the lowered third in the minor triad.

Major and Minor Triad Exercise

2. Practice major and minor five-finger patterns and triads in Technique Exercise 4 in this chapter.

MINOR TRIAD

The **minor triad** includes a *minor third* (three half steps) between the root and the third, a *major third* (four half steps) between the third and the fifth, and a *perfect fifth* (seven half steps) between the root and the fifth.

A minor triad   *D minor triad*

Performing Minor Triads in Block-Chord Form

Practice the minor triad in *block-chord form* in the following positions at the keyboard. Use the hand-over-hand technique when specified, and strive for a legato sound between chords. Try these positions with other minor triads.

Block-Chord Exercise: Minor Triad

Part A

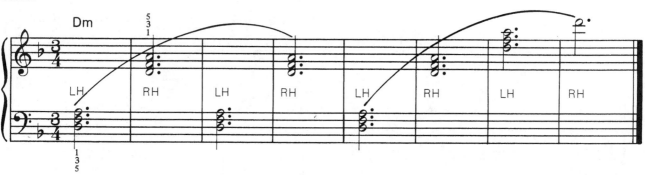

Part B

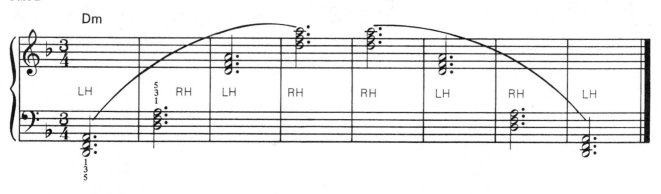

Performing Minor Triads in Arpeggio Form

Practice the minor triad in the broken-chord, or arpeggio, form. Again, connect chord tones as smoothly as you can. Try these positions with different minor triads.

Arpeggio Exercise: Minor Triad

Part A

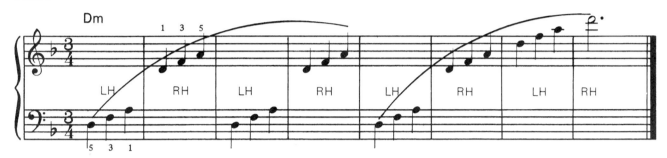

Part B

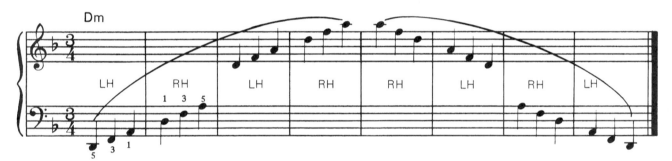

TONIC CHORD (MINOR)

The first pitch of the minor five-finger pattern is called the tonic, and the chord built on the first step is called the *tonic chord* or i. The tonic chord for the minor pattern is a minor triad. (Lowercase roman numerals are often used for minor triads.)

D minor five-finger pattern—Tonic chord

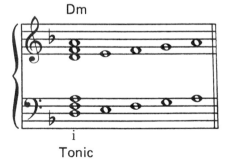

Tonic Chord and Minor Five-Finger Pattern

Locate the tonic triad for each minor five-finger pattern. Play the following exercise in these minor five-finger patterns: D, A, E; and C, G, F.

D minor

Performing Melodies with Minor Triad Accompaniment

The following minor melodies are accompanied with the minor triad or use the minor triad as part of the accompaniment. Analyze each before playing. Determine the minor pattern and triad; then play both. Notice the interval relationship between notes. Be sure to keep your eyes on the music. Transpose to other minor patterns.

Bulgarian Folk Melody

Allegro

Folk Melody 7

Adagio

Israeli Folk Melody 2

Moderato

Polish Folk Melody

RHYTHM

Rhythm Exercise: $\frac{2}{3}$ $\frac{3}{4}$ $\frac{4}{4}$ ♩ ♩. ♩ ♩. ♫ ♬ ♬ 𝄽 𝄾 Clap, chant, or play the following examples on any key(s), or any chord. Check the number of beats per measure and the number of beats or fraction of beats each note and rest receive.

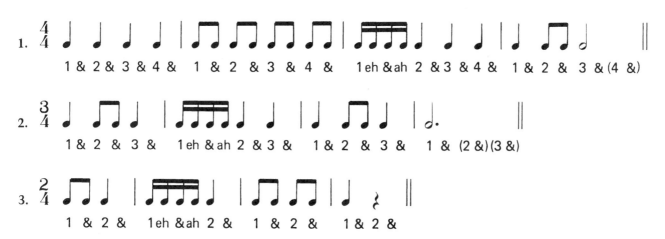

COMPOSING PROJECT

Minor-Triad Composition

Create a parallel-phrase melody based on a minor triad.

Step 1. Choose a minor triad on which to base your piece. Identify the three pitches in the triad. Play those pitches with both hands.

Step 2. Using those three pitches, create an eight-measure melody that includes two parallel phrases. (Refer to Chapter 4 to review parallel phrases.) Experiment with various pitches and rhythms until you decide on something that pleases you. You may divide the melody equally between the two hands or play the melody in one hand and add a triad accompaniment in the other. Be sure to conclude your melody on the root of the triad.

Step 3. Notate your composition on the staff below, and then play, reading from staff notation. Exchange your melody with a classmate's, and assess each other's work for accuracy and creativity.

ENSEMBLE PLAYING

Chapter 5 Ensemble Pieces:

1. Duet Exercise 42, pp. 288–289
2. "It's Natural to Have a Flat," pp. 290–291

REPERTOIRE

Visually analyze the following pieces. What can you say about the intervals between pitches? Are there definite phrases? If so, are they parallel, contrasting, or something different? What about the tempo and the dynamics? Look up information about Van de Vate in Biographical Sketches of *PianoLab* Composers (Appendix M) and Van de Vate's and Kunz's places in the history of music in the Timeline (Appendix K). Choose one of the pieces to memorize.

"A Quiet Exchange" falls within an E-to-B white-note five-finger pattern. This pattern is not major or minor but part of the Phrygian mode (see Chapter 10). Notice how the material in the first four measures appears in opposite hands in the second four measures (called *invertible counterpoint*). Move the RH up one octave when repeating this piece. Play as softly as possible.

A Quiet Exchange

Moderato   Nancy Van de Vate (United States, b. 1930)

In "Canon,"* notice the imitation of the RH melody in the LH. This piece
falls within the E minor five-finger pattern. Practice hands separately and then
hands together.

Canon   Konrad Max Künz (Germany, 1812–1875)

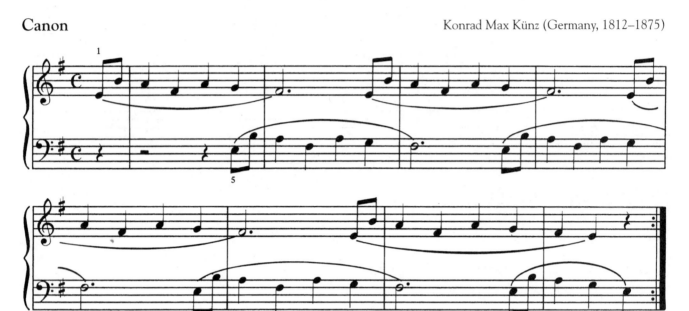

TECHNIQUE EXERCISES

Check your keyboard position and your hand position.

Exercise 1: Contrary Motion Keep your wrists flexible and your arms moving in
a gentle outward and upward movement for each two-measure pattern in Part A.
When you arrive at the whole note, look ahead to what comes next so you'll be
ready. In Part B, the arm movements will be reversed. Transpose this exercise to
the minor patterns of G, A, D, E, B, and F.

Part A

*A **canon** is a composition in which all parts have the same melody but start at different times.

Part B

Exercise 2: Intervals (Minor Five-Finger Pattern) Play these intervals in the following pattern. Stress independent finger action, and work for a legato sound. Transpose to other minor five-finger patterns.

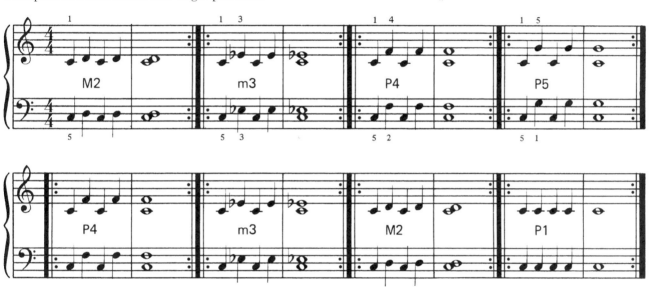

Exercise 3: Consecutive Thirds Practice this exercise slowly with each hand separately and with hands together. Connect the thirds as smoothly as possible. Change to other major and minor patterns.

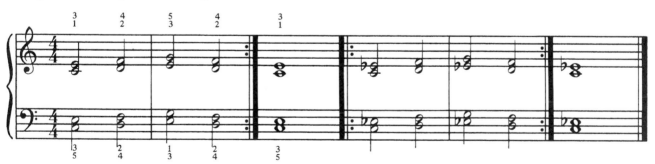

Exercise 4: Parallel Motion The major and minor five-finger patterns and major and minor triads are explored in this exercise. Be attentive to independent finger action on the major and minor pattern. Transpose to the major and parallel minor patterns of G, A, D, E, B, and F.

Exercise 5: Extension Fingering The five-finger pattern is extended to cover six pitches instead of five in this major and minor exercise. Play without accidentals (in parentheses) for the C major pattern and with accidentals for the C minor pattern. Practice for clarity and accuracy. Transpose to other major and minor patterns.

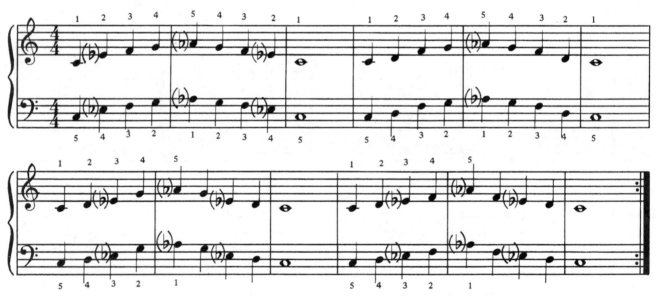

CHAPTER EVALUATION

1. Build and play a minor five-finger pattern on the following tonics: C, D, E, F, and G.

2. Using the A minor pattern, play major seconds, minor thirds, and perfect fourths and fifths.

3. At the keyboard, transpose Czech Folk Melody 1, on p. 91, from D minor to C minor.

4. Demonstrate a minor triad on any given root, and identify the minor third and the perfect fifth. Contrast a major triad with a minor triad at the keyboard.

5. Perform by memory one of the pieces in this chapter.

6. Demonstrate extension fingering by performing Technique Exercise 5 in this chapter.

7. The whole-step–half-step arrangement of the minor five-finger pattern is as follows:

   1 __(whole)__ 2 _____ 3 _____ 4 _____ 5

8. Notate the following minor five-finger patterns on the staff and keyboard chart. When accidentals are needed, write the sharps or the flats on the staff *before* the pitches on the *same* line or in the *same* space.

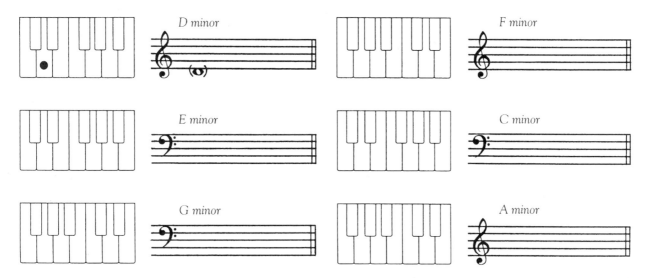

9. Label the following intervals by quality and number (for example, m3). Underneath this identification, specify the number of half steps in each interval. Use the preceding keyboard charts to help in visualizing the half steps.

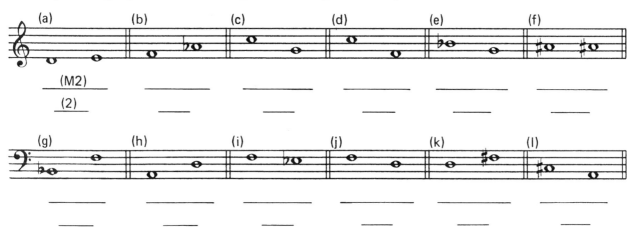

10. Write minor triads on the following roots.

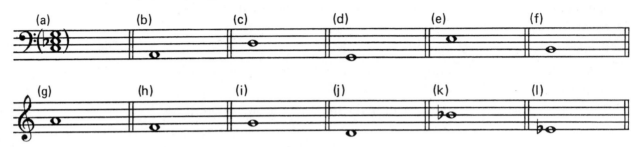

11. Describe the following terms:

    a. Minor five-finger pattern

    b. Minor triad

    c. Block chord

    d. Arpeggio

12. Identify the following musical symbols:

    a. ♪♪♪♩

    b. Cm, Dm, Em

    c. m3

    d. P4

    e. M2

6

Major Scales

Major Key Signatures

Tonic and Dominant Chords

Crossover/Cross-under Fingering

Thumb-Under Technique

Staccato Touch

MELODY

INTRODUCTION TO SCALES

The word **scale** comes from the Latin word *scala,* meaning ladder. In music of Western civilization, scales can be identified by particular interval patterns. The two scale forms most familiar to us are the *major* and the *minor scales,* but the pentatonic, the whole-tone, the blues, and many other scales and modes also serve as the pitch framework for much of the world's music.

The Major Scale

The pattern of the **major scale** includes five whole steps and two half steps.

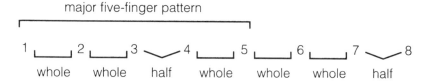

The major scale pattern is illustrated by the white keys on the keyboard from C to C.

C major scale

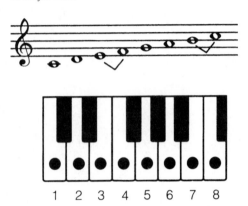

Performing the C Major Scale

1. Say or sing the letter names as you play the C major scale. Use the **tetrachord** (succession of four pitches), or two-handed, fingering. Notice the important pull of the seventh step (B) toward the eighth step (C).

C major scale

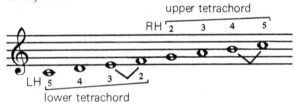

2. Play the descending C major scale at the beginning of "Joy to the World."

Isaac Watts

Joy to the World (excerpt)   George Frideric Handel (Germany, 1685–1759)

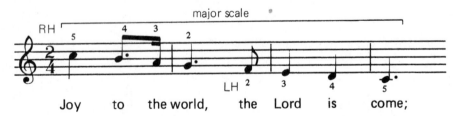

3. Play "St. Paul's Steeple" using the tetrachord fingering. (Play also as a **round** with four groups, each group starting after the first two notes of the previous group.)

St. Paul's Steeple

American Folk Melody

The major scale without alterations is referred to as **diatonic.** Major scales may begin on any of the twelve available pitches, and as long as the whole-step–half-step pattern (the diatonic pattern) is reproduced exactly, the characteristic sound will be the same. The only major scale that has no sharps or flats is C.

IDENTIFICATION OF SCALE TONES

Scale Degrees

Each pitch, or degree, of the major scale has a specific name.

Major scale degrees

Syllable Names

Pitches may be identified by letters, numbers, degree names, and *syllable names.* Seven syllable names—do, re, mi, fa, sol, la, ti—are often used to identify pitches in a scale.

C major scale and syllables

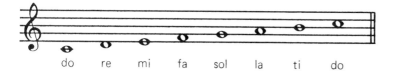

In the song "Do-Re-Mi" from the musical *The Sound of Music*, syllables are used as part of the lyrics. Sing the syllable names while playing the scale sequence in the final measures of "Do-Re-Mi."

Oscar Hammerstein II (United States, 1895–1960)
Richard Rodgers (United States, 1902–1979)

Do-Re-Mi (excerpt)

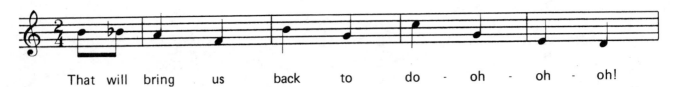

That will bring us back to do - oh - oh - oh!

do - re - mi - fa - sol - la - ti - do!

MAJOR KEY SIGNATURES

The sharps or the flats needed to create the various major scales are placed at the beginning of each staff of music (right after the clef sign). This grouping of the sharps and flats is called a **key signature.**

Any sharp or flat in the key signature applies to the corresponding note in all octaves. For example, if a B-flat is in the key signature, then all B's (whether in bass or treble clef or in any position on the staff) must be performed as B-flats.

Placement of Sharps and Flats

The sharps and the flats in the key signature are placed in a specific order. The order of sharps is F C G D A E B.

The order of flats if B E A D G C F. Notice that the order of flats is the reverse of the order of sharps.

Order of sharps

Order of flats

Guidelines for Determining the Tonic or Major Key

Step 1. Determine whether the key signature uses sharps or flats.

Step 2. If the key signature includes *sharps*, locate the sharp farthest to the right. This is scale tone 7, and the next line or space above (one half step above) is the key or the tonic.

Step 3. If the key signature includes *flats*, there are two ways to determine the tonic or major key. One way is to simply identify the next-to-the-last flat in the key signature—that pitch is the tonic. (With this approach, you need to memorize that the key of F has one flat.) The other way is to locate the flat farthest to the right (scale tone 4) and count down to 1 (the tonic).

Sharp key signatures

Flat key signatures

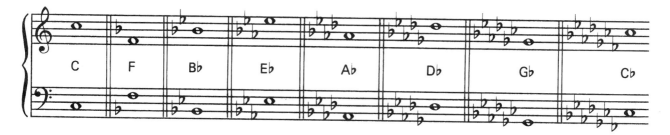

Circle of Fifths

The fifteen major scales and key signatures can be arranged in a sequence called the **circle of fifths.** Moving clockwise *up* the interval of a perfect fifth to the tonic, you can see that each new key adds one more sharp. Moving counter-clockwise *down* a perfect fifth, you can see that each key adds one more flat. Three keys are enharmonic: B and C♭, F♯ and G♭, and C♯ and D♭.

Enharmonic Keys

Performing Major Scales (Tetrachord Fingering)

1. Perform the following major scale tetrachord exercise. This exercise will help you learn the major scale patterns with sharps. Begin with the C major scale two octaves below middle C, and play in tetrachord position. Then place your LH on the upper tetrachord of the C major scale (G A B C), making this the lower tetrachord of the G major scale. Remember to cover the RH notes quickly with the LH. (Notice that your RH fourth finger always plays the new sharp.)

Major Scale Tetrachord Exercise: Sharp Keys

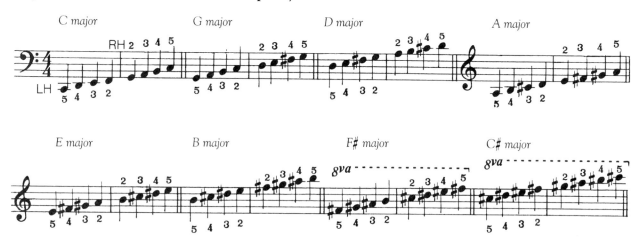

2. Perform the following major scale tetrachord exercise with scales that include flats. Begin with the C♭ major scale (two octaves below middle C), and play in tetrachord position. Again place your LH on the upper tetrachord of the C♭ major scale (G♭ A♭ B♭ C♭), making this the lower tetrachord of the G♭ major scale. Notice that your RH fourth finger always "drops" a flat from the previous scale.

Major Scale Tetrachord Exercise: Flat Keys

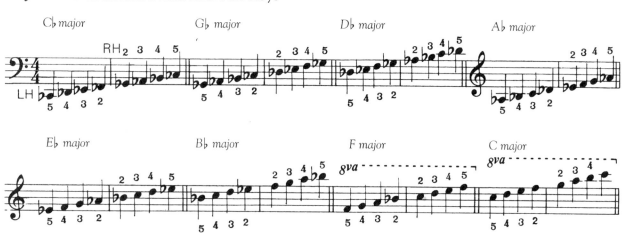

Identifying Major Keys

Determine the major key for the following pieces. Use the guidelines to help in the identification.

> **Guidelines for Identifying Major Keys**
>
> **Step 1.** Examine the key signature to determine the tonic or key.
>
> **Step 2.** Identify the final pitch in the piece. Most often, that pitch will be the tonic.
>
> **Step 3.** The results of steps 1 and 2 will most likely be the same, and therefore, the major key has been identified.

Wiengenlied   Daniel Gottlob Türk (Germany, 1750–1813)

Hush Little Baby   American Folk Song

INTERVALS

Eight intervals are created between the tonic and the eight ascending degrees of the major scale. The seconds, thirds, sixths, and sevenths are always major intervals; the unisons, fourths, fifths, and octaves are always perfect.

Intervals in Major Scale

C major

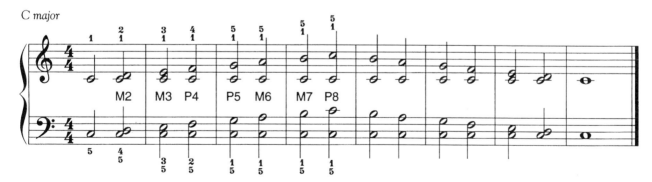

Interval Exercises

1. Read and play each interval in the major scale. Feel the distances and listen to the sound of each interval.

2. Play these intervals in the following exercise. Practice hands separately and hands together. Transpose to other major scales.

Major Scale Interval Exercise

3. Practice these intervals in Technique Exercise 3 in this chapter.

MAJOR SCALE (ONE-HAND FINGERING)

To play a major scale with one hand, you must cross fingers over and under other fingers. The major scales are fingered in several ways. One-hand fingerings for all major scales are in Appendix D. The fingering for the C major scale (also the same for the G, D, A, and E scales) is as follows:

C major scale

Performing Major Scales (One-Hand Fingering)

1. Practice the following thumb-under exercise in preparation for one-hand scale playing. In this exercise, the thumb will tuck under to move as smoothly as possible to the next pitch. The thumb needs to do all the work; the hands and arms stay relaxed and without movement. Play this exercise hands separately first and then hands together. Continue the pattern until you reach the upper C.

Thumb-Under Exercise in Major

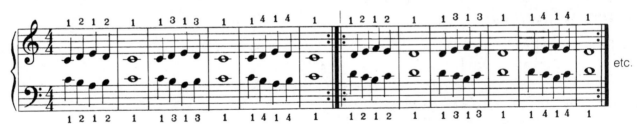

2. Practice the C major scale with one-hand fingering in two octaves in contrary motion. Practice hands separately, then hands together. Notice that the fingering is the same in the two hands.

C major scale in contrary motion

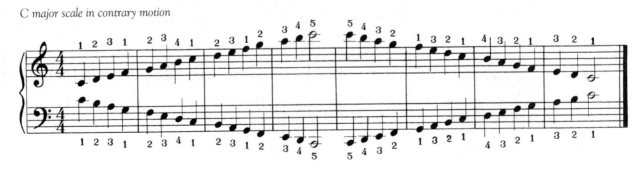

3. Practice the C major scale with one-hand fingering in two octaves in parallel motion (p. 114). Practice hands separately and, when the fingering is secure, hands together.

4. Once the fingering is secure for the C major scale, try the G and D major scales in contrary motion and in parallel motion.

G major scale

D major scale

5. Practice Technique Exercise 1 in this chapter.

Performing Major Scale Melodies (One-Hand Fingering)

1. This South American folk melody uses all the pitches in the major scale. Use the one-hand fingering with the RH. What is the range of the LH part?

South American Melody

2. "The First Noel" is a more challenging scale melody. Practice the RH one-hand fingering. Look only at the music, even when your thumb moves under. Feel the movement. Perform by yourself or with another pianist. (One pianist can play the RH melody while another plays the bass line. At one piano, a pianist can play the bass line as written with the LH or the RH while another plays the melody an octave higher.)

The First Noel   Carol

3. For even more challenging scale melodies, try "Joy to the World," p. 271, and the excerpt from "Hymne" by Vangelis, p. 264.

HARMONY

TONIC AND DOMINANT CHORDS

The most important chord in the scale is the tonic (I), and second in importance is the **dominant** or V. In a major scale, both the I and the V are major chords. The tonic triad includes pitches 1, 3, and 5 of the major scale, and the dominant triad includes pitches 5, 7, and 2.

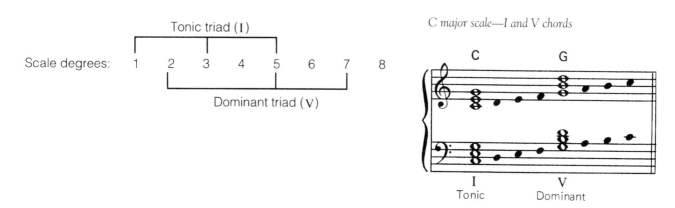

Authentic Cadence

Since I conveys the strongest sense of arrival, most melodies conclude on the tonic pitch or chord. Because two of the pitches (7 and 2 of the major scale) in the V chord have a tendency to "pull" toward the I, the V is often followed by the I. When a phrase, section, or piece concludes with the V–I progression, the closing, or **cadence,** is called **authentic.**

Authentic cadence

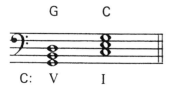

Op. 117, No. 10

Con moto   Cornelius Gurlitt (Germany, 1820–1901)

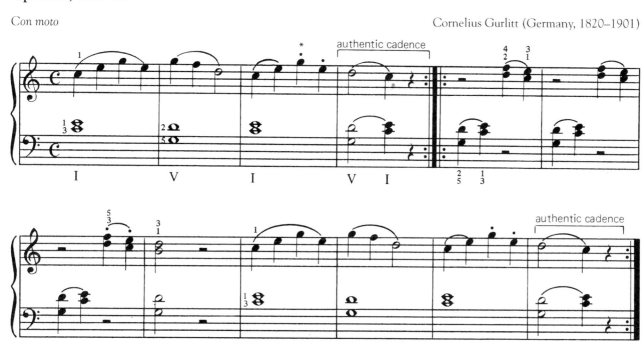

*A dot above or below a notehead indicates that the tone should be disconnected and shortened. See Technique Exercise 2 at the end of the chapter.

Dominant Seventh Chord

The dominant (V) chord is not always a triad. Quite often it includes four notes and is called a **dominant seventh chord** (V7).* The V7 is represented in lead sheet notation by a capital letter plus a 7—for example, C7, G7, F7.

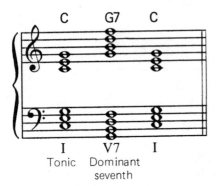

"Piano Position" for V7 Chord When one chord progresses to another, it is important to find tones that are common to both or tones that are closest to each other. This simplifies the fingering, avoids awkward sounds, and allows the chord tones to move smoothly one to another.

To simplify the moves between the I and the V7 chords, the fifth of the V7 chord is sometimes omitted and the other tones are rearranged or inverted. This is often called the "piano position."

The common tone in the I and the V7 chords is the top one, so those pitches in the two chords stay the same. As you move from the I to the V7 chord, the middle note of the I chord moves up a half step and the bottom note moves down a half step, forming the V7 chord inversion.

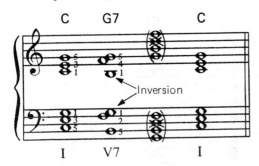

The RH fingering of the **V7** chord in piano position is $\frac{5}{4}$.

The LH fingering of the **V7** chord in piano position is $\frac{1}{2}$.

*More information on seventh chords is found in Chapter 8.

I and V7 Chords in Selected Major Keys

Practice the I and the V7 chords in the following frequently used major keys (all chords and fingerings are in Appendix G). Develop a feel for this progression and be ready to change chords.

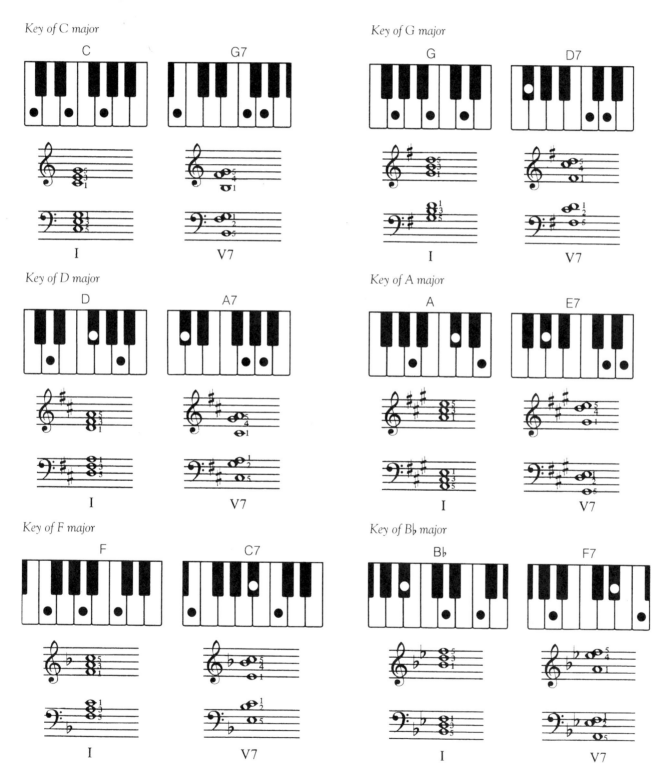

Performing I–V7 Chords

1. Perform the following exercise to practice the necessary moves between the two chords. Part A prepares the hands for the moves between the two chords in Parts B and C. Transpose this exercise to all major keys.

I–V7 Exercise

Part A

Part B

Part C

2. Perform the following pieces using the I and the V7 chords. Review the rhythm, melody, and form of each before playing. Transpose to other major keys.

The Cuckoo

German Folk Song

English Folk Melody 3

Andante

August Eberhard Müller (Germany, 1767–1817)

Other melodies to accompany with the I and the V7 chords:

"Little River," p. 54

"Jim-Along Josie," p. 54

Israeli Folk Melody 1, p. 78

Chilean Folk Melody, p. 55

COMPOSING PROJECT

I and V7 Melody

Create a two-phrase melody that uses the pitches in the I and the V7 chords.

Step 1. Select a major key of your choice, and identify the pitches in the I and the V7 chords for that key.

Step 2. Use the following chord progression for the eight-measure melody. Experiment with various rhythms, using the pitches in the designated chords. Unify your composition with repetition, and incorporate contrasting ideas for variety.

Phrase 1:   I | V or V7 | I | V or V7 |
Phrase 2:   I | V or V7 | V or V7 | I   ‖

Step 3. Create an accompaniment to go with your melody. You can use chord roots, block chords, broken chords, or any member of the chord.

Step 4. Notate your melody and accompaniment on a staff, and then play, reading from staff notation. Exchange your melody with a classmate's. Play your pieces for each other, and assess your work for accuracy and creativity.

ENSEMBLE PLAYING

Chapter 6 Ensemble Pieces:

1. Etude, Op. 82, Nos. 10 and 11, pp. 292–293
2. "Come, Follow," p. 293

REPERTOIRE

Analyze each of the following pieces. Choose at least one to memorize. Look up information about the composers (Appendix M) and their places in the history of music (Appendix K).

Eighteenth-century composers generally did not include touch, dynamic markings, and the like in their music. But the touch for "March" (Türk) would most likely be the "normal" one of the eighteenth century—*nonlegato*. Türk indicates in his *Klavierschule* book (1789) that "for those notes which are to be played in the normal touch, one lifts each finger off the key a bit earlier than the actual note values may indicate."

March

Daniel Gottlob Türk (Germany, 1750–1813)

In the Gurlitt composition, a dialogue between the RH and the LH is featured. Practice in four-measure segments, hands together.

Study for Two

Con moto   Cornelius Gurlitt (Germany, 1820–1901)

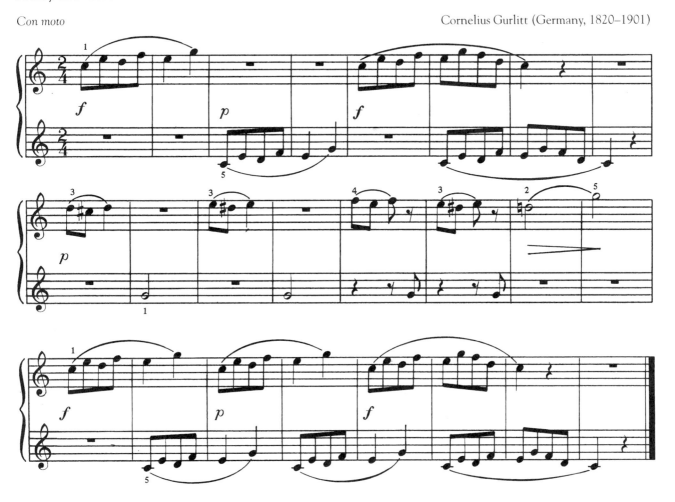

A **duet** is usually a composition to be performed by two people. This piece is a
"duet" for just one person; actually, the duet is performed by the player's left and
right hands.

A Duet (No. 2 from *First Term at the Piano*)

Moderato   Béla Bartók (Hungary, 1881–1945)

TECHNIQUE EXERCISES

Exercise 1: Thumb-Under This thumb-under exercise requires the thumb to
tuck under several fingers. Again, try to move as smoothly as possible. Keep the
hand in position, and keep the hands and arms relaxed. Make the thumb do all the
work. Play this exercise in many different major patterns.

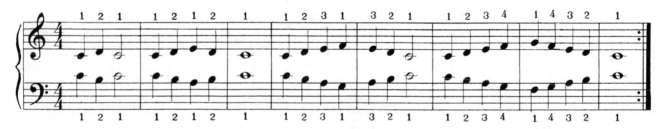

Staccato Touch

Staccato touch requires playing in a detached style. In notation, the staccato mark
(𝅘𝅥 or 𝅘𝅥𝅮) appears above or below the notehead to indicate that the tone should be
disconnected and shortened. Staccato playing is the opposite of legato playing.

   To get a feel for the wrist action important in staccato touch, knock with your
knuckles on the keyboard lid or the top of the piano. Be sure to knock with your

wrist loose and your arm not moving. Once this knocking action is secure, tap first with your index finger (2), gradually adding the middle (3) and the ring (4) fingers.

Exercise 2: Staccato Touch Transfer this knocking wrist action to the keyboard by playing the following examples hands separately with the staccato touch. Strike each key with a precise motion from the wrist only. Release the key immediately. Keep your wrist loose but your arm still.

Part A

Part B

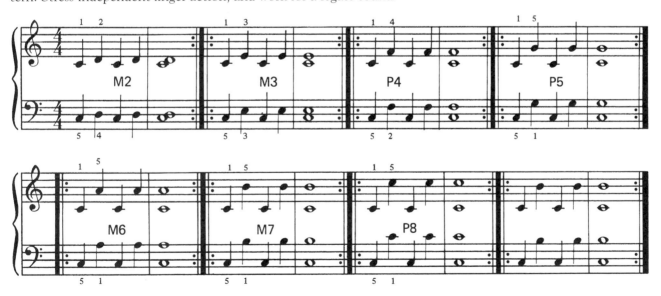

Exercise 3: Intervals (Major Scale) Practice these intervals in the following pattern. Stress independent finger action, and work for a legato sound.

CHAPTER EVALUATION

1. Demonstrate the major scale pattern and key signatures by playing the tetrachord exercises in this chapter.

2. At the keyboard, transpose "St. Paul's Steeple" (earlier in this chapter) from C major to D major.

3. Using the C major scale, play and identify these intervals: major second, major third, perfect fourth, perfect fifth, major sixth, major seventh, and perfect octave.

4. Demonstrate the one-hand fingering (two octaves) for the G major scale.

5. Play I and V7 chords (with the V7 rearranged in "piano position") in any major key. Demonstrate smooth hand shifts.

6. Perform one of the pieces in the Repertoire section accurately and musically. Be able to discuss the characteristics of its melody, rhythm, and form.

7. Write the whole-step–half-step arrangement of the major scale:

    1 (whole) 2 _____ 3 _____ 4 _____ 5 _____ 6 _____ 7 _____ 8

8. Construct major scales, ascending and descending, on the following tonics. Write the letter name, the number, and the syllable (do, re, and so on) under each pitch. When accidentals are needed, write the sharps or the flats *before* the pitches on the *same* line or in the *same* space.

(a)

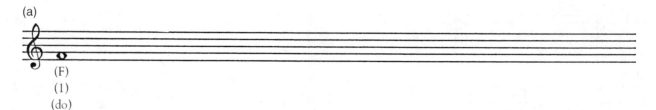

    (F)
    (1)
    (do)

9. Identify the following scale degrees by letter name.

   a. The tonic of the E♭ major scale is _____.

   b. The dominant of the F major scale is _____.

   c. The leading tone of the D major scale is _____.

   d. The subdominant of the G major scale is _____.

   e. The supertonic of the B♭ major scale is _____.

   f. The mediant of the A major scale is _____.

   g. The submediant of the C major scale is _____.

10. Notate the tonic for each major key as determined by the key signature.

11. Write the key signatures for the designated keys. Be sure that the flats and the sharps are in the correct order, are in the appropriate lines or spaces, and are not crowded. Refer to the key signature chart on p. 108.

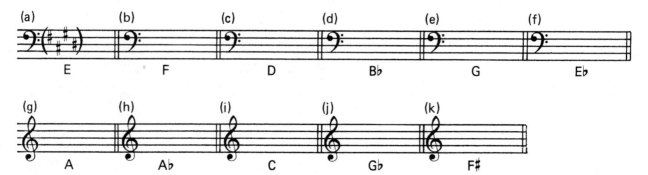

12. Complete the following:

    a. The key of F major has _____ flats.

    b. The key of D major has _____ sharps.

    c. The key of E major has _____ sharps.

    d. The key of B♭ major has _____ flats.

    e. The key of A major has _____ sharps.

    f. The key of E♭ major has _____ flats.

    g. The key of G major has _____ sharps.

13. Label the following intervals by quality and number.

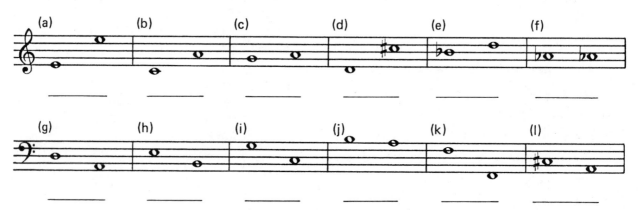

14. Construct the tonic (I) and the dominant (V or V7) chords on the appropriate scale degrees.

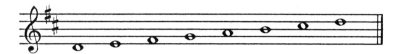

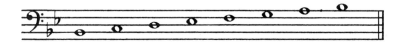

15. Describe the following musical terms:

   a. Major scale

   b. Tetrachord

   c. Syllable names

   d. Key signature

   e. Circle of fifths

   f. "Piano position" for I and V7 chords

   g. Crossover/cross-under fingering

   h. Staccato touch

16. Identify the following musical symbols:

   a. ♩

   b. V7

   c. G7

   d. P8

   e. M7

   f. M6

7

Primary Chords

Twelve-Bar Blues Progression

Syncopation

A B and A B A Form

Legato Pedaling

Drop/Lift Technique

HARMONY

PRIMARY CHORDS

The I (tonic) and the V (dominant) chords were presented in Chapter 6. By adding the IV (subdominant) chord, we have identified the **primary chords.** These are the three most frequently used chords in tonal music.

The **subdominant** chord is built on the fourth degree of the scale and, like the I and the V chords, is a major triad in a major key. The IV chord includes pitches 4, 6, and 8 (1) of the major scale.

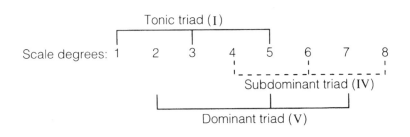

Primary chords in C major

Tonic   Subdominant   Dominant

Plagal Cadence

The tonic triad is always the last chord in a final cadence. When the tonic triad is preceded by a subdominant chord, the result is a **plagal cadence** (IV–I).

Plagal cadence

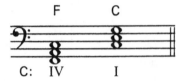

Tar Paper Stomp*

Wingy Manone (United States, 1904–1982)

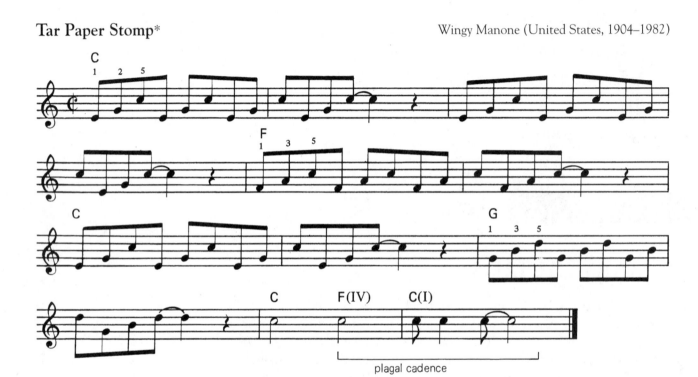

plagal cadence

Performing Primary Chords

1. Practice the following exercise, which changes between these three chords. Play in the designated block-chord form and in arpeggio form. Transpose to other major scales.

*The big-band hit "In the Mood" was based on "Tar Paper Stomp."

Block-Chord Exercise: I–IV–V

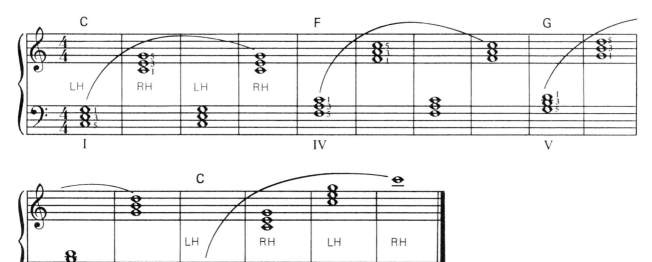

2. Practice Technique Exercise 2 at the end of this chapter. Try the technique described there with the preceding Block-Chord Exercise. Hold the pedal down until a new chord is indicated.

3. Perform the chords in "Tar Paper Stomp" with your LH while the instructor or more experienced players perform the RH melody. Notice that the entire melody consists of pitches in each of the three chords.

TWELVE-BAR BLUES PROGRESSION

The traditional twelve-bar **blues** (twelve measures) can be played using the primary chords. The chord order for one version of the twelve-bar progression follows.

    I I I I   IV IV I I   V IV I I

Practice the blues progression in C major. At first you might play just the root of each chord; then play all the pitches in the chords. Develop a feel for the distances so you do not have to look down at the keys. Bring RH 1 to RH 5; LH 5 to LH 1 quickly when moving from the I chord to the V chord. Reverse the process in moving from V to I.

Twelve-bar blues progression

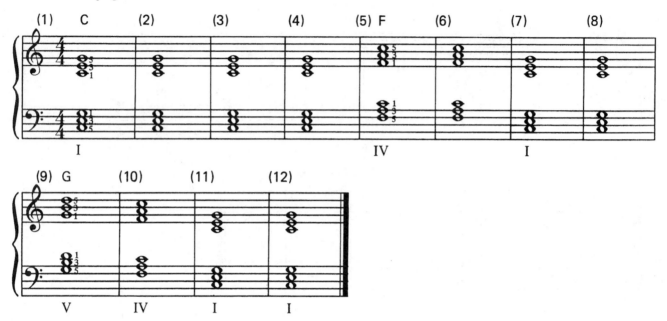

To create a RH melody based on the blues progression, you can play the tones in each chord one at a time. Practice "Chordal Blues" looking at the music, not at your hands. Continue to feel these chord jumps. When you are comfortable with the piece, vary the rhythm and the order of chord tones to create a new version.

Finally, transpose "Chordal Blues" to primary chords in other major keys.

Chordal Blues

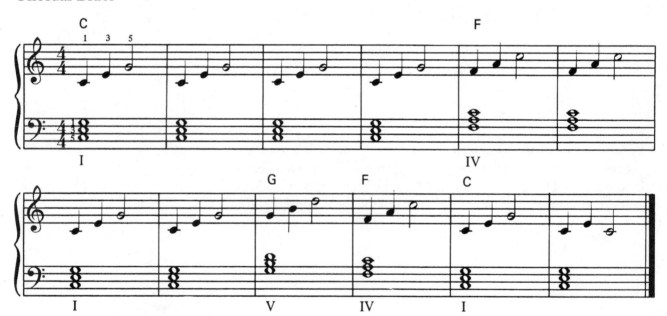

Performing Blues Compositions

1. "Plain Blues" incorporates **blue notes** (lowered thirds of each chord). (The natural sign— ♮ —cancels a flat or a sharp.) Use the same fingering for each chord. Notice the *accent marks* (>) on beat 2 in each measure—stress this note and a more "bluesy" flavor will result.

Plain Blues

2. In "Leftie Blues," the LH plays the individual chord tones and blue notes (an octave lower than written) while the RH plays the block chords. Notice the accent mark on beat 2—again, observe the result.

Leftie Blues

3. "Amanda's Blues" features a steady eighth-note rhythm in the RH. Keep your wrist loose as you perform the eighth notes. The LH "walks" through the chord tones and the blues notes an octave lower than written.

Amanda's Blues

Amanda Herbert

© 1980, Amanda Hebert. Used by permission.

Amanda Hebert composed this blues piece while enrolled in a beginning piano and music fundamentals course at San Francisco State University.

4. More blues pieces may be found on pp. 139, 150, 218, 255, and 256.

R H Y T H M

SYNCOPATION

Syncopation is a rhythmic device that gives variety and interest to all kinds of music. It is integral to jazz and occurs in the music of many cultures around the world.

Syncopation is the placement of accents on weak beats or offbeats. It may be likened to putting an accent on the wrong syllable in language. In "Plain Blues," on page 135, and "Leftie Blues," on page 136, accents are placed on a weak beat in each measure. This creates syncopation.

Nonsyncopated Major Scale Example The following scale example is notated in 4/4, which indicates that the strong beats (beats 1 and 3) will be slightly accented and the weak beats (beats 2 and 4) will not be accented. Play the scale making those accented notes slightly louder than those without accents.

C major scale (with accents on 1 and 3)

Syncopated Major Scale Example The following scale example is noted in 4/4. However, in this example, the weak beats (2 and 4) are accented, which creates syncopation. Play the scale accenting the weak beats.

C major scale (with accents on 2 and 4)

Syncopation may be created by omitting an accent where one is expected as well as by placing one where it is not expected. When a rest is placed on a strong beat, the accent may be shifted to a weak beat.

Rhythm Exercise: Syncopation—accented offbeats, omitted accents (rests)

Performing Syncopated Melodies

"Shabat, Shalom" includes accents on offbeats to create syncopation. Clap the rhythm of the melody before playing. The RH part falls within the D minor five-finger pattern (D E F G A).

Shabat, Shalom (excerpt)

Hebrew Song

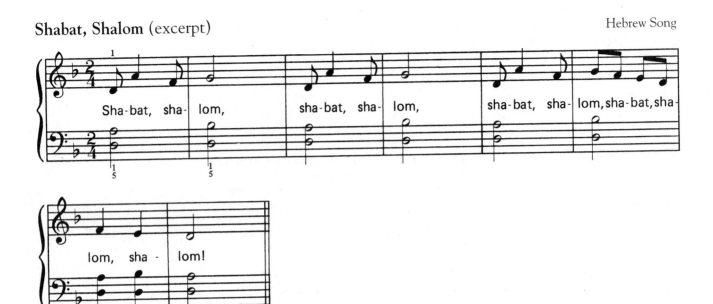

"Syncopated Blues" creates syncopation by placing a rest on the first beat of each measure. Clap the rhythm of the RH part before playing.

Syncopated Blues

Other melodies in major keys that include syncopated rhythms:

"Hey Lidee," p. 270
"Tom Dooley," p. 159
"Hello! Ma' Baby," p. 295

FORM

SECTIONAL FORM

In longer pieces of music, phrases are combined and organized into *sections*. Some pieces can be divided into two or three sections. Pieces with two sections are referred to as *two-part* (**A B**) or **binary form,** whereas three-section pieces are **ternary** (**A B A**).

A B (Binary) Form

"Dance" is an example of A B, or binary, form. The second section (beginning in measure 9) requires good finger action with the RH. Practice this exercise before playing the piece. What is the range of the RH part in this piece?

Dance

Cornelius Gurlitt (Germany, 1820–1901)

A B A (Ternary) Form

"Funny Dialogue" has three sections (A B A). Notice how the rhythmic *motives* (brief musical ideas) ♩ ♫ ♩ and ♫♫ ♩ are manipulated and used to unify. Clap these rhythms first; then practice a section at a time. This could also be performed with another player (one on RH and one on LH).

Funny Dialogue

Allegretto   Dmitri Kabalevsky (Russia, 1904–1987)

Determine the formal design (A B or A B A) for the following pieces:

"Bourrée" by L. Mozart, p. 243

"Mazurka" by Szymanowska, p. 252

"We Three Kings," p. 198

"Hey Lidee," p. 270

COMPOSING PROJECT

Blues Piece

Create a piano blues piece based on the twelve-bar progression.

Step 1. Choose a flat key, such as F major, to use for your blues piece. Determine the three primary chords for that key as well as the blue note for each chord.

Step 2. On staff paper, prepare a skeleton of your composition by blocking out the twelve measures (or bars) on the grand staff and notating the appropriate chords in each measure. Also indicate the blue note for each.

Step 3. Using your twelve-bar chord progression, experiment with the pitches in the designated chords and the blue notes. A meter of 4/4 is a good place to start with rhythm. Try to incorporate some syncopation, too.

Step 4. When you have finalized your ideas, notate your blues piece, and then play, reading from staff notation. Exchange your blues piece with a classmate's. Play your pieces for each other, and assess your work for accuracy and creativity.

ENSEMBLE PLAYING

Chapter 7 Ensemble Pieces:

1. "Hello! Ma' Baby," pp. 294–295
2. "Blue Jeans," pp. 296–297

REPERTOIRE

Study the Bartók piece and identify the five-finger pattern used in both hands. Does the first phrase use parallel or contrary motion between hands? Notice the legato and staccato markings. Practice Technique Exercise 3 in this chapter before playing the piece.

Morning Song (No. 5 from *First Term at the Piano*)

Moderato

Béla Bartók (Hungary, 1881–1945)

What do you notice about phrases 1 and 2 in "Up or Out"? Note the change in dynamics and the register change of the RH in phrase 2.

Up or Out

Moderato

Nancy Van de Vate (United States, b. 1930)

What is the sectional form for this Beethoven piece? What can you say about the phrases? Practice one section at a time.

Russian Folk Song, Op. 107, No. 3

Ludwig van Beethoven (Germany, 1770–1827)

TECHNIQUE EXERCISES

Exercise 1: Independent Hands and Hand Coordination Establish a good hand position. Practice this exercise with good finger action. Feel the weight of your arm shift from one finger to the next. Connect pitches as smoothly as possible. Transpose to other major keys.

Pedaling

When the **damper pedal** (located to the far right) is pressed down, pitches can be sustained to produce a legato effect. This depressing of the pedal releases the felt dampers from the strings and permits the strings to vibrate freely. (Look inside the piano to see what happens when you play a note and depress the damper pedal.)

To use the damper pedal, rest the ball of the foot lightly on the pedal, keeping your heel on the floor. Practice depressing and releasing the pedal. Check that your heel does not leave the floor. Listen for any mechanical noises—you should pedal with as little noise as possible. A marking in music for the damper pedal is as follows:

down   up-down   up

Play a note, depress the damper pedal, then remove your finger from the key. Listen to the continuing sound. Repeat this exercise until you can smoothly and quickly play a note and immediately depress the pedal.

Exercise 2: Legato Pedaling To legato-pedal, you must learn to connect several notes or chords with the pedal. To do this, you must play a note, depress the pedal, play another note releasing the pedal, and immediately depress again.

Try this exercise connecting one pitch to the next without a break. Listen carefully to make sure the pedal has sustained only one note. Clear pedaling is the goal.

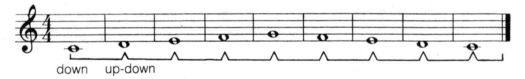

down   up-down

Perform the primary chords in C major adding the legato pedaling. Transpose the primary chords to other major keys.

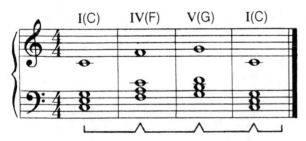

Exercise 3: Drop/Lift Practice these two-note slurs with action mainly from the wrist. Elevate the wrist a bit, and as you play the first note, drop the wrist to key level with a slight bounce. On the second note, lift the wrist to the original position. Keep your fingers firm. Transpose to other major keys.

CHAPTER EVALUATION

1. Play I, IV, and V chords (in root position) in the keys of C, G, D, F, and B♭.

2. At the keyboard, improvise a blueslike piece using primary chords in the twelve-bar blues progression.

3. Demonstrate legato pedaling with the primary chords in Technique Exercise 2 in this chapter, or in the I–IV–V exercise earlier in the chapter.

4. Demonstrate understanding of syncopation by performing one of the lines in the rhythm exercise in this chapter.

5. Memorize and perform a piece in A B or A B A form.

6. Write the I, IV, and V chords (in root position) for the following major keys.

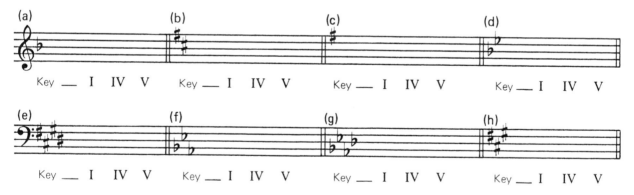

7. Identify the primary chords by letter name for the twelve-bar blues progression in B♭ major.

I (____) I (____) I (____) I (____)

IV (____) IV (____) I (____) I (____)

V (____) IV (____) I (____) I (____)

8. Notate possible pitches for a melody line as indicated by the LH chords in each measure.

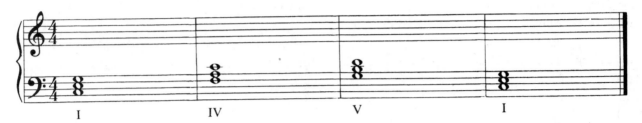

       I   IV   V   I

9. Describe the following musical terms:

    a. A B form

    b. Syncopation

    c. Blue note

    d. A B A form

    e. Primary chords

    f. Plagal cadence

10. Identify the following musical symbols:

    a.

    b. I IV V

    c. *8va sempre*

    d. ⌞___∧___∧___⌟

8

Dominant Seventh Chord

Chord Inversions/Figured Bass

Nonchord Tones

Harmonization

Compound Meter

Alberti Bass

HARMONY

SEVENTH CHORD

The **seventh chord** includes four notes: a triad with an added third. There are several kinds of seventh chords, but the one frequently used in *PianoLab* is the *major-minor seventh chord*. This chord, also commonly referred to as the **dominant seventh chord,** includes a major triad with an added seventh above the root.

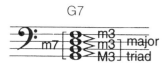

Performing Major-Minor Seventh Chords

"Seventh Chord Blues" and "Seventh Chord Boogie" both include open sevenths (m7) in the LH part. Determine what the other chord tones would be in each of the seventh chords. "Boogie Rock" includes complete seventh chords in the RH part.

Seventh Chord Blues

Seventh Chord Boogie

Boogie Rock

CHORD INVERSIONS

Triads and seventh chords are not always written in root position (the root of the chord positioned as the lowest pitch). Chord tones may be rearranged, or *inverted*.

The triad has two **inversions.**

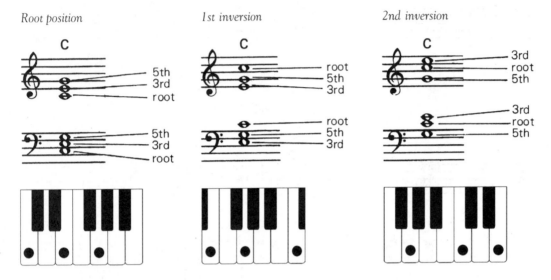

The seventh chord has three inversions.

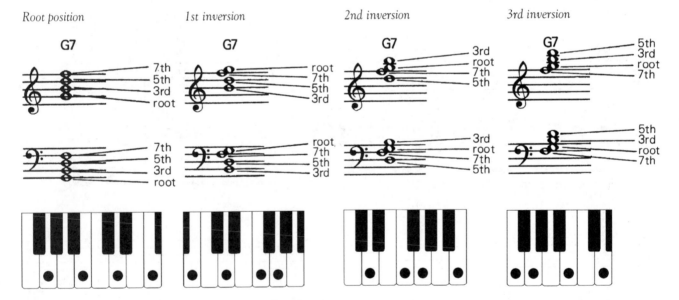

Chord Inversions with Figured Bass

Arabic numerals are sometimes added to roman numerals to indicate specific chord inversions, as in V7. The use of arabic numerals originated in the *figured bass* system of the *Baroque period* (c. 1600–1750), when keyboard players were skilled in improvising elaborate compositions from a given series of pitches and numerals (figures).

The numerals show intervals within the chord and are measured from the lowest (bass) note to the other notes in the chord. Parentheses identify numbers not commonly shown but understood to be in the chord.

Figures for triads

Triad	Arabic numerals
Root	none
1st inversion	6
2nd inversion	$\frac{6}{4}$

(5)   6   6
(3) (3) 4

Figures for seventh chords

Seventh chord	Arabic numerals
Root	7
1st inversion	$\frac{6}{5}$
2nd inversion	$\frac{4}{3}$
3rd inversion	$\frac{4}{2}$

7   6 (6) (6)
(5) 5   4   4
(3) (3) 3   2

Chord Inversions for Keyboard Playing

To make the hand and finger moves easier between two or three chords, some chords are performed in inversions. These inversions allow the hand to stay in one position and play two or three chords.

I AND IV⁶₄ CHORDS

Of the two inversions of the IV triad, the second inversion (IV⁶₄) is the closer to the tonic (I) in root position. Notice how the bottom notes stay the same for the two chords while the middle note moves up a half step and the top note moves up a whole step.

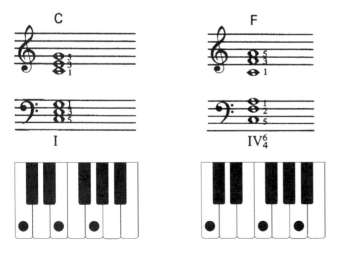

I–IV⁶₄ Chords in Selected Major Keys

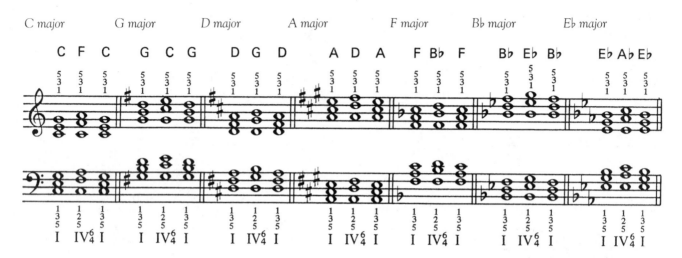

Performing I–IV⁶₄ Chords

1. Perform Part A of the following exercise, which prepares the hands for the I–IV⁶₄–I fingerings.

2. Perform Parts B and C of the I–IV⁶₄ Exercise to practice the necessary moves between the two chords. Transpose to other major keys.

I–IV⁶₄ Exercise

Part A

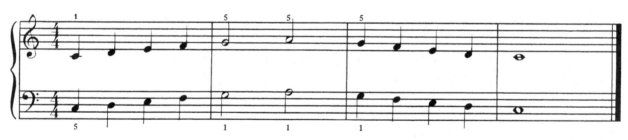

Part B

Part C

3. Perform "Lovely Evening" using these chords for an accompaniment. First, practice in the usual block-chord style; then try the broken-chord accompaniment shown here.*

Lovely Evening†

Traditional Round

4. Practice Technique Exercise 1 at the end of this chapter. This exercise stresses contrary motion and the arpeggio style.

NONCHORD TONES

Harmony (chords) and melody are related. For example, in Chapter 7, the melody of "Tar Paper Stomp," page 132, is made up entirely of pitches in the primary chords, and the blues pieces are based primarily on chord tones.

---

*Other broken-chord patterns are notated in Appendix H.

†Perform as a round with several groups of pianos. Piano 1 begins the melody. Piano 2 enters when Piano 1 begins measure 7 (2). Piano 3 begins the melody when Piano 2 has reached measure 7. Repeat as many times as desired. (At one piano, one pianist can play Piano 1 part an octave higher while another plays Piano 2 part an octave lower.)

Although the framework of a melody is mostly chord tones, other pitches are added between them. These tones are called *nonchord tones*.

Passing tones and **neighboring tones** are two kinds of nonchord tones. They often fall on unaccented beats (2 and 4 in quadruple meter; 2 in duple; and 2 and 3 in triple) or on unaccented parts of beats.

Passing tones (p.t.) come between pitches that are a third apart.

Neighboring tones come stepwise between repeated pitches and can be either upper neighbors (u.n.) or lower neighbors (l.n.).

In the following melody, the I (F) and the V7 (C7) chords serve as the chord framework. The circled pitches are nonchord tones. Label the nonchord tones as p.t. and u.n. or l.n. and perform.

Melody 1 (with nonchord tones circled)

Identifying Nonchord Tones

1. Analyze the following melodies (based on the I and the V7 chords) for non-chord tones. Circle and label the p.t. and the u.n. or l.n. Perform each.

   "Whistle Daughter," p. 79

   Folk Melody 6, p. 78

   Israeli Folk Melody 1, p. 78

   "The Cuckoo," p. 121

2. Add nonchord tones—p.t. and u.n. or l.n.—to the following chordal melody. Place the nonchord tones on unaccented beats or on unaccented parts of beats. Alter the rhythmic durations as needed, and rewrite on the staff below. Perform the melody with chordal accompaniment. Notate the accompaniment.

Melody 2

I AND V⁶₅ CHORDS

In Chapter 6 rearranging the chord tones of the dominant seventh chord (V7) made for a smoother move from the I to the V7. The first inversion (V⁶₅) is commonly used when playing the I and the V7 because it is the closest to the tonic in root position. Notice how the top notes stay the same for the two chords while the middle note of the V⁶₅ moves up a half step and the bottom note moves down a half step.

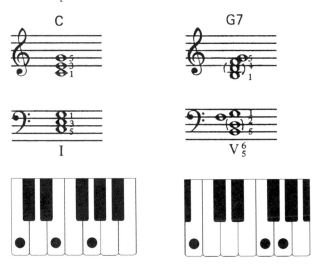

I and V⁶₅ Chords in Selected Major Keys

Practice the I and the V⁶₅ chords with the RH and LH in the following frequently used major keys (all chords are in Appendix G). Try to develop a feel for this progression, and be ready to change chords.

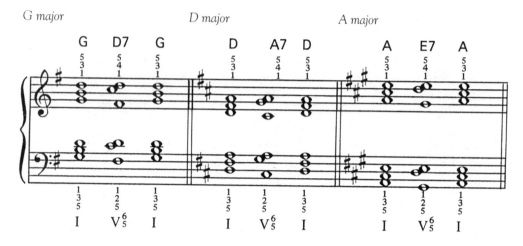

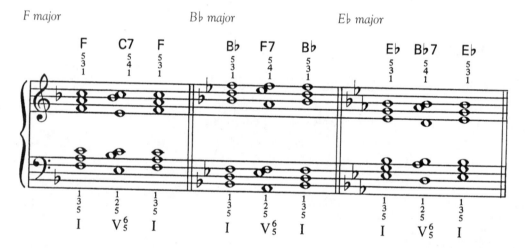

Performing I–V⁶₅ Chords

1. Review the I–V7–I exercise on p. 120.

2. Perform the following pieces using the I–V⁶₅ for an accompaniment. Transpose to other major keys.

Mary Ann

Calypso Song

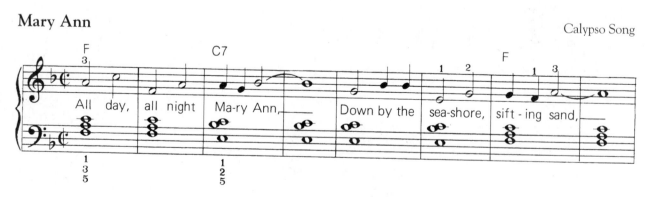

Tom Dooley   American Folk Song

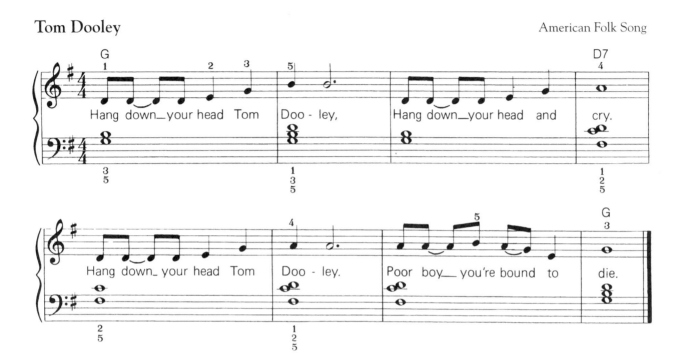

I, IV$_4^6$, AND V$_5^6$ CHORDS
IN SELECTED MAJOR KEYS*

Key of C major

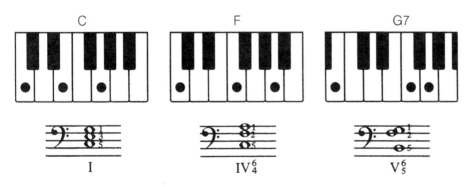

*I, IV, and V7 chords for all major keys are notated in root position and in I–IV$_4^6$–V$_5^6$ form in Appendix G.

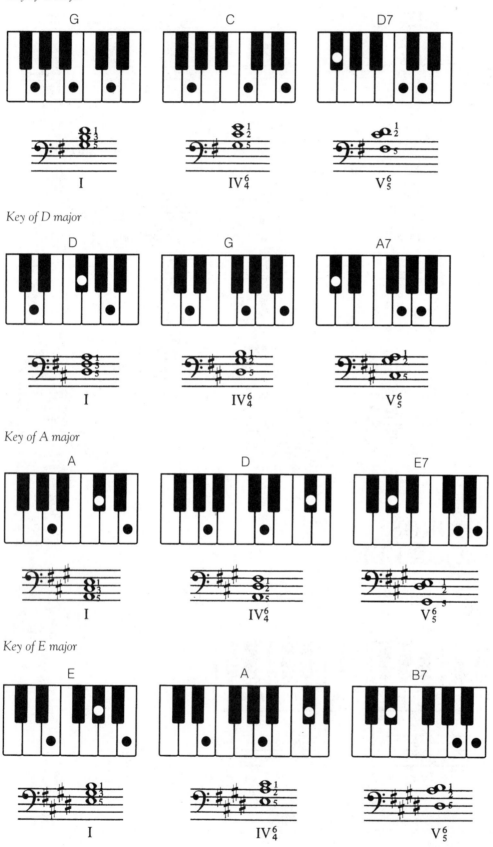

Key of F major

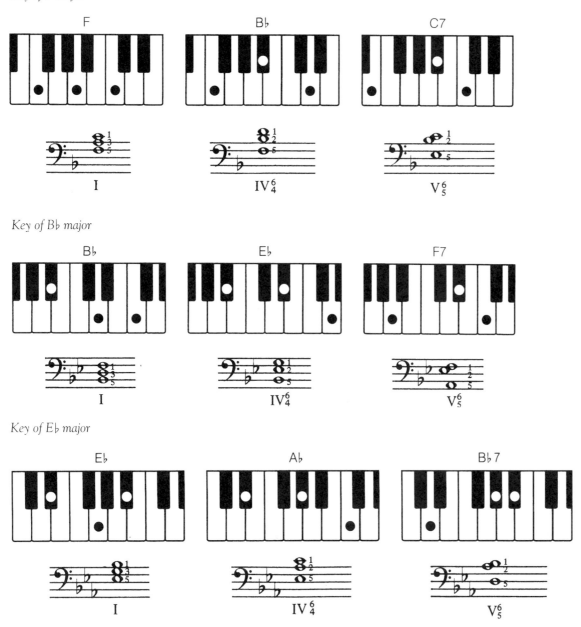

Performing I–IV$^6_4$–V$^6_5$ Chords

1. Perform the following exercises to practice the moves between the three chords. The fingerings and the whole-step–half-step moves will be the same in any major key. Memorize this progression. Learn to shift quickly and smoothly from one chord to another. Feel the shape of the next chord, and actually touch the keys just before playing. Transpose these exercises to other major keys.

I–IV$_4^6$–V$_5^6$ Exercise

Part A

Part B

Part C

2. Use legato or syncopated pedaling for the next exercise of the primary chords. Try not to blur chord tones or overlap sounds of single notes. Connect evenly when crossing hands. Transpose to other major keys.

Arpeggio Exercise: I–IV$_4^6$–V$_5^6$

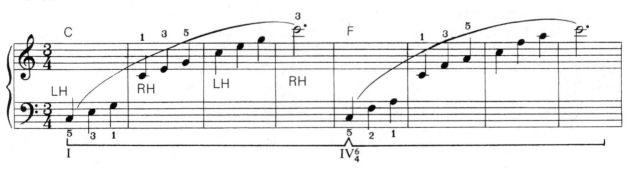

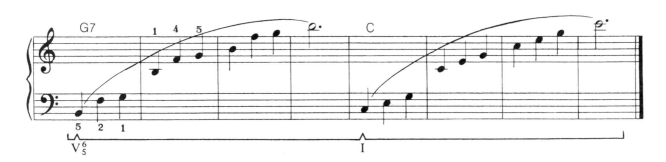

3. Perform the following pieces. Determine the major key and the primary chords first; then practice the chord progression. Be sure to review the rhythm, form, fingering, and so on for each piece before performing. Transpose to other major keys.

Drink to Me Only with Thine Eyes (excerpt)   English Folk Song

Banks of the Ohio   American Ballad

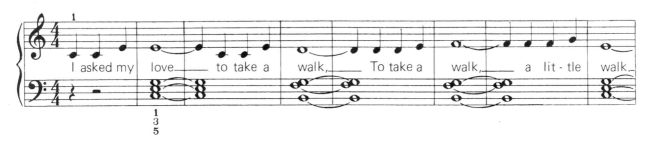

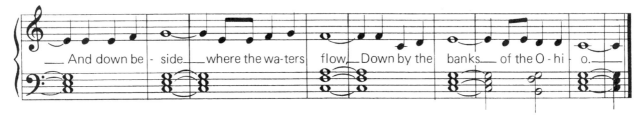

Amen (excerpt)

Refrain   African-American Spiritual

A - - men, A - men, A - men, A - men, A - men.

Bohemian Christmas Carol

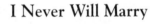

I Never Will Marry

American Folk Song

I nev-er will mar-ry___ I'll be no man's wife___ I in-

tend to live sin - gle___ All the days of my life.___

4. The following songs can be accompanied with the I, IV, and V7 chords.

"The First Noel," p. 116

"Joy to the World," p. 271

"Amazing Grace," p. 271

"De Colores," p. 274

"John B," p. 272

HARMONIZATION

Selecting appropriate chords for a melody is referred to as **harmonization.** To select appropriate chords, determine what chord(s) matches pitches in the melody.

> **Guidelines for Harmonizing Melodies**
>
> **Step 1.** Determine the key of the melody and the pitches in the I, IV, and V7 chords for that key.
>
> **Step 2.** For each measure, compare the pitches in the melody with the pitches in the three chords. Decide which chord (or chords) includes *most* of the pitches in that measure. (The first pitch in the measure and the pitches on the other strong beats are especially important in making this choice.) Many melodies can be harmonized with one chord per measure, and others may need two or more. (There may be a few pitches in the melody that are not in the three chords—these pitches are referred to as nonchord tones.) If the melody begins on an upbeat, the upbeat is usually not chorded. Also remember that a melody normally ends on the tonic pitch and the tonic chord.
>
> **Step 3.** Try the chosen chords with the melody. It is important to *always check each musical decision by playing at the keyboard.* Write the roman numerals or the letter names for the selected chords above or below each measure of the melody. (Or notate the correct chords in root position or in the I–IV$^6_4$–V$^6_5$ position below the melody—see the "Tante Minna" example.)

Tante Minna (harmonized)

Example: C major (I = C E G, V7 = G B D F)   German Folk Melody

Harmonizing Melodies

Harmonize the following melodies. Play the harmonizations, and notate the melodies and the chords on a staff. (A staff is provided for German Folk Melody 3 only.)

German Folk Melody 3

The Cradle

Austrian Carol

English Folk Melody 4

French Canadian Round*

*Peform "French Canadian Round" with two groups of pianists. Piano 1 begins. Piano 2 enters when Piano 1 has reached measure 3. Repeat as many times as desired. (At one piano, a pianist can perform Piano 1 part an octave higher while another performs Piano 2 part an octave lower.)

Capriccio in G Major (excerpt)

Franz Joseph Haydn (Austria, 1732–1809)

On Top of Old Smoky

American Folk Melody

Lullaby

Johannes Brahms (Germany, 1833–1897)

Kum Ba Yah

African-American Song

R H Y T H M

COMPOUND METERS

All the meters studied so far are classified as simple, and in simple meter the beat is divided into two equal parts. When the beat divides into three equal parts, the meter is referred to as **compound.**

Simple   *Compound*

Selected Meter Signatures (Compound Meter)

In compound meter, the beat is represented by a dotted note, which divides into three equal parts. Since there is no number to designate a dotted note, the bottom number of a compound meter signature shows divisions of the beat and the top number shows how many divisions in a measure. The top number is always a multiple of three: To determine the meter (duple, triple, quadruple), divide the top number by three.

Compound duple meter

6 — 6 beat divisions per measure   6
8 — ♪ is the value of each division   8   1 2 3 4 5 6

Compound triple meter

9 — 9 beat divisions per measure   9
8 — ♪ is the value of each division   8   1 2 3 4 5 6 7 8 9

Compound quadruple meter

12 —12 beat divisions per measure   12
8 — ♪ is the value of each division   8   1 2 3 4 5 6 7 8 9 **10** 11 12

Rhythm Exercise: Compound Meter Compound meters may be counted several ways. One way is to count the division values of the beat stressing 1 and 4 (7 and 10). A second way is to say a sound such as "eh" and "ah" on the second and third division of each group of three.

Performing Pieces in Compound Duple Meter

1. Determine the number of beats each note receives, and clap the rhythm of each piece before playing. Transpose each to other major keys.

Flemish Folk Melody

Fiddle Dee Dee

English Folk Melody

For He's a Jolly Good Fellow

French Folk Song

2. For more challenging compound meter examples, perform the following
   pieces:

   "Silent Night" p. 262

   "Promenade" (Bielawa), p. 172

   "Memory" from *Cats* (excerpt), p. 269

   Theme from 6 Variations (Beethoven), p. 247

*DC al fine (Da capo al fine) means to return to the beginning and conclude with the measure marked fine.

COMPOSING PROJECT

Two-Phrase Melody

Create a two-phrase melody based on the following major chord progression:

| *Phrase 1:* | I | | I | | V7 | | V7 | |
| *Phrase 2:* | I | | I | | V7 | | I | || |

Step 1. Decide which major key you wish to use for your melody, and determine the I and the V7 chords in that key.

Step 2. On staff paper, prepare a skeleton of your melody by blocking out the eight measures and notating the appropriate chords in both treble and bass clefs.

Step 3. Decide on a meter signature and then experiment with the pitches in the designated chords. You might want to limit yourself to quarter and half notes and use only chord tones for the melody part. Your accompaniment could include block chords in the I and the V_3^6 positions or be varied to suit the melody.

Step 4. Notate your melody and accompaniment on the staff, and then play, reading from staff notation. Exchange your melody with a classmate's. Play your pieces for each other, and assess your work for accuracy and creativity. Are the phrases of your melody parallel or contrasting?

ENSEMBLE PLAYING

Chapter 8 Ensemble Pieces:

1. Study (from Op. 823), pp. 298–299
2. "Linus and Lucy" excerpt, pp. 298–299

REPERTOIRE

What is the sectional form of Diabelli's piece? Any similar phrases?

Melody

Moderato   Anton Diabelli (Austria, 1781–1858)

Visually analyze "Promenade" for rhythmic features. What is the meter? Notice that this contemporary piece has some new sounds and combinations of sounds. The composer describes the piece as being "freely tonal with chromatic color tones inserted."

Promenade

                                                    Herbert Bielawa (United States, b. 1930)

Notice the perfect fifth intervals in the LH and the thirds and fourths in the RH. Block out the interval positions before performing the piece.

Saturday Smile

So casual

Lynn Freeman Olson (United States, 1938–1987)

Kabalevsky uses the F major, G minor, and G major triads in this piece. Practice the RH triads in block form and with tones one at a time. Practice LH block chords; notice the added F in the G minor and G major triads.

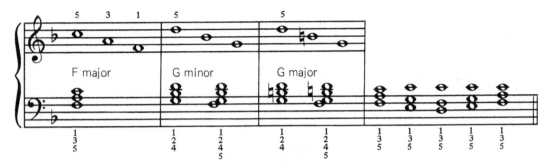

A Little Dance, Op. 39, No. 9

Allegro molto   Dmitri Kabalevsky (Russia, 1904–1987)

TECHNIQUE EXERCISES

Exercise 1: Contrary Motion and Arpeggio Practice the following exercise using arpeggios. Keep the wrists flexible and the arms moving in a gentle outward and upward movement. Transpose to other major keys.

Exercise 2: Extension Fingering This Hanon exercise requires the fingers to expand to the six-finger position (fingers 1 and 2 skip a note between them) and focuses on the stretch between the fifth and the fourth fingers of the LH ascending and the fifth and the fourth fingers of the RH descending. Begin practicing slowly, lifting the fingers high and playing each note with precision. Gradually increase the speed.

The Virtuoso Pianist, No. 1 (simplified version)   Charles Louis Hanon (France, 1820–1900)

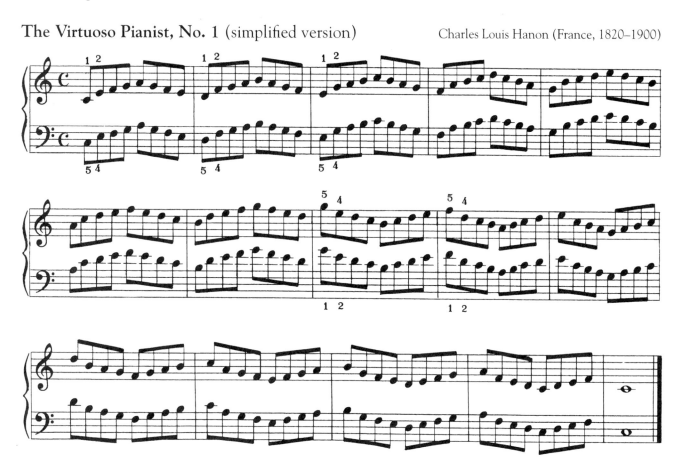

Exercise 3: Broken Chord (Alberti Bass) Practice the following two studies
for facility in using the broken-chord figure in both hands. This particular figure
when performed in the bass is often called the **Alberti bass.** (Eighteenth-century
composer Domenico Alberti used these figures in his sonatas.)

Part A

Part B

CHAPTER EVALUATION

1. Play the primary chords in the I–IV$_4^6$–V$_3^6$ position in the following major keys
    with correct fingering: C, G, D, A, E, F, B♭, E♭, A♭.

2. Demonstrate legato pedaling by performing the exercise on p. 162.

3. Harmonize one of the melodies on pp. 166–167 with primary chords.

4. Play with rhythmic accuracy a piece in this chapter that has a compound me-
    ter.

5. Construct major-minor seventh chords (dominant seventh chords) on the
    given roots.

(a)   (b)   (c)   (d)   (e)   (f)   (g)   (h)

6. Label these major triads and major-minor seventh chords as follows: root position (R), first inversion (1st), second inversion (2nd), or third inversion (3rd).

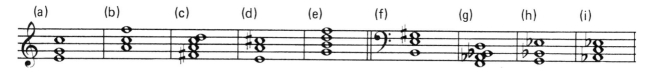

7. Write the primary chords for the stated key in root position and then in the I–IV$_4^6$–V$_5^6$ position.

8. Harmonize Melody 3 and Melody 4 with the appropriate chords. Notate the chords on the staff below the melody. Write the chords in the I–IV$_4^6$–V$_5^6$ position.

Melody 3

Key: _____

Melody 4

Key: _____

9. Write a meter signature in compound duple meter _____, compound triple meter _____, and compound quadruple meter _____.

10. Create and notate a rhythmic phrase in the specified meters and lengths. Use a variety of note possibilities.

$\begin{smallmatrix}6\\8\end{smallmatrix}$ | | | ‖

$\begin{smallmatrix}9\\8\end{smallmatrix}$ | | | ‖

11. Describe the following musical terms:

    a. Dominant seventh chord

    b. Root-position chord

    c. Chord inversions

    d. Figured bass

    e. Nonchord tones

    f. Harmonization

    g. Compound meters

12. Identify the following musical symbols:

    a. IV_4^6

    b. V_5^6

    c. $\frac{12}{8}$

9

MELODY

THE MINOR SCALES

The major and minor scales are the scale patterns that serve as the basis for most **tonal music.** Major scales have one pattern, whereas **minor scales** *come in three forms: natural minor, harmonic minor, and melodic minor.* Each form has a particular pattern of whole and half steps. All three forms have in common a half step between the second and the third scale degrees.

major five-finger pattern

Major: 1 2 3 4 5 6 7 8

minor five-finger pattern

Natural minor: 1 2 3 4 5 6 7 8

Harmonic minor: 1 2 3 4 5 6...7 8 $1\frac{1}{2}$

Melodic minor: 1 2 3 4 5 6 7 8 7 6 5 4 3 2 1

179

NATURAL MINOR SCALE

The **natural minor scale** (probably the oldest form of the minor scale) includes five whole steps and two half steps. The half steps occur between steps 2 and 3 and steps 5 and 6. The natural minor scale pattern is represented by the white keys from A to A.

A natural minor scale

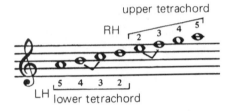

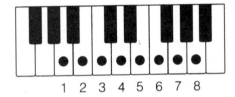

Performing the Natural Minor Scale

1. Practice the A natural minor scale with the tetrachord fingering. Pay close attention to the whole and half steps.

2. Sight-read "Hatikvah" with the tetrachord fingering.

Hatikvah (excerpt)

Israeli National Anthem

3. Perform the following piece, which uses pitches in the D natural minor scale. The RH stays within the minor five-finger pattern.

Melody, Op. 39, No. 3 (from *24 Little Pieces*)   Dmitri Kabalevsky (Russia, 1904–1987)

Natural Minor Scale (One-Hand Fingering)

Crossover and cross-under fingering is needed to play the natural minor scale with one hand. The fingering for the A natural minor scale (also the same for E, D, G, and C minor scales) is as follows:

A natural minor scale

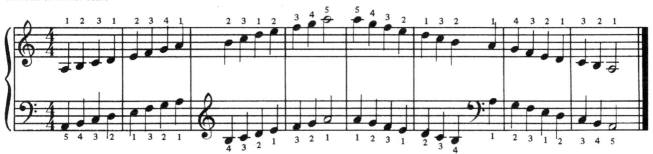

Performing the Natural Minor Scale (One-Hand Fingering)

1. Practice the following thumb-under exercise in preparation for one-hand minor scale playing. Keep the hand in position and let the thumb do all the work.

Thumb-Under Exercise in Minor

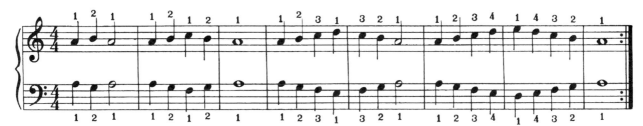

2. Perform the above A natural minor scale with one-hand fingering in two octaves—in contrary motion and in parallel motion.

MINOR KEY SIGNATURES

Relative Major and Minor Key Signatures

The minor key signatures may be related to major key signatures, for each major key shares a key signature with a minor key. Major and minor scales with the same key signature are referred to as **relative.**

The key signatures and the tonics are the same for natural, harmonic, and melodic minor scales. However, the natural minor is the only form that uses the pitches indicated by the key signature exclusively.

Relative major and minor key signatures

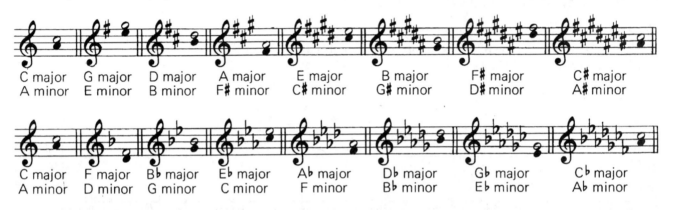

C major	G major	D major	A major	E major	B major	F♯ major	C♯ major
A minor	E minor	B minor	F♯ minor	C♯ minor	G♯ minor	D♯ minor	A♯ minor

C major	F major	B♭ major	E♭ major	A♭ major	D♭ major	G♭ major	C♭ major
A minor	D minor	G minor	C minor	F minor	B♭ minor	E♭ minor	A♭ minor

Guidelines for Determining the Tonic or Minor Key

Step 1. To identify the tonic or minor key, it is easiest to first locate the major tonic.

Step 2. Count down three half steps (or a minor third) from the major tonic to determine the minor tonic or key. (When a major tonic is in a space, the minor one is in the next lower space. When a major tonic is on a line, the minor one is on the next lower line.)

The Circle of Fifths

The fifteen minor key signatures progress in a sequence of perfect fifths. This sequence can be arranged in a circle of fifths, as the major keys are. By moving clockwise *up* the interval of a perfect fifth to the tonic, each new key adds one more sharp. By moving counterclockwise *down* a perfect fifth, each new key adds one more flat. The three enharmonic keys appear at the bottom of the circle.

Enharmonic Keys

HARMONIC MINOR SCALE

The **harmonic minor scale** is the most frequently used. It is the form upon which chords (harmonies) are usually built. The harmonic minor scale has the same half steps between 2 and 3 and 5 and 6 as the natural minor but raises the seventh degree one half step, creating a step and a half between 6 and 7. (The raised seventh also establishes a half step between 7 and 8, as in the major scale.) The raising of the seventh tone is accomplished by an accidental rather than by a change in the key signature. The key signature is the same for natural minor and harmonic minor.

A harmonic minor scale

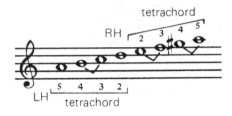

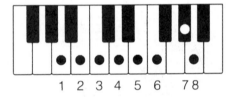

Performing the A Harmonic Minor Scale (Tetrachord Fingering)

1. Practice the A harmonic minor scale with the tetrachord fingering. Be conscious of the whole and half steps, and listen for that familiar "pull" from 7 toward 8.

2. Perform Israeli Folk Melody 3, which uses the A harmonic minor scale. Notice that the G♯ (seventh step) is added in the music.

Israeli Folk Melody 3

3. Perform the following harmonic minor scale tetrachord exercises.

Harmonic Minor Scale Tetrachord Exercise—Sharp Keys Beginning with A minor, build harmonic minor scales at the keyboard using the tetrachord fingering. Follow the LH-over-RH format used in the tetrachord fingering of major scales. For example, place your LH on the upper tetrachord of the A minor scale (E F G♯ A), making this the lower tetrachord of the E harmonic minor scale. Remember to cover the RH notes quickly with the LH.

A harmonic minor   *E harmonic minor*

Harmonic Minor Scale Tetrachord Exercise—Flat Keys Beginning with the A♭ minor scale, build harmonic minor scales using the tetrachord fingering. Follow the same LH-over-RH format.

A♭ harmonic minor   *E♭ harmonic minor*

Harmonic Minor Scale (One-Hand Fingering)

The harmonic minor scales have different one-hand fingerings.* The fingering follows for the A harmonic minor scale (also the same for the E, D, G, and C minor scales).

*One-hand fingerings for all minor scales are shown in Appendix E.

A harmonic minor scale

Performing the Harmonic Minor Scale (One-Hand Fingering)

1. Practice the above A harmonic minor scale with one-hand fingering in two octaves—first in contrary motion and then in parallel motion.

2. Once the fingering is secure for the A minor scale, try the E, D, G, and C minor scales.

MELODIC MINOR SCALE

Of the three forms of minor, the **melodic minor** is used the least. This scale has the same half steps between 2 and 3 as natural and harmonic but raises both the sixth and the seventh pitches one half step. The melodic minor usually descends in the natural minor form. (As with the harmonic form, if the raising of the sixth and seventh steps requires an accidental, this is added in the melody, not in the key signature.)

A melodic minor scale

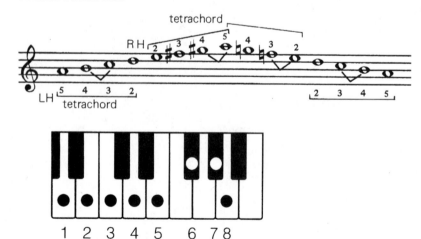

Melodic Minor Scale (One-Hand Fingering)

The one-hand fingering for the A melodic minor scale follows. This fingering is the same for the E, D, G, and C melodic minor scales.

A melodic minor scale

Performing the A Melodic Minor Scale

1. Practice the A melodic minor scale, first with the tetrachord fingering and then with the one-hand fingering (two octaves). Listen to the raised sixth and seventh ascending and the return to natural minor in the descending portion.

2. Measures 2 and 3 of "Yesterday" are based on the A melodic minor scale. Notice the raised sixth and seventh in the melody. Play this portion of the song with the RH. (The entire song is on p. 277.)

John Lennon (England, 1940–1980)
Paul McCartney (England, b. 1942)

Yesterday (excerpt)

Yes-ter-day, all my trou-bles seemed so far a-way,

IDENTIFICATION OF SCALE TONES

Scale Degrees

The degrees of the minor scales are identified by the same names as those of the major scale—with the exception of the seventh in the natural minor form. Since the natural minor scale does not have a half step between the seventh and the eighth degrees, the seventh degree is often referred to as the **subtonic.**

Minor scale degrees

Syllable Names

Pitches in the minor scales may be referred to with syllable names, just as in major. Two approaches are used for associating syllables with pitches in minor keys.

1. Scales begin with *do* as in major, and the remaining syllables are altered when necessary. This approach stresses the relationship of the sound of the tonic with the syllable *do*.

2. Scales begin with *la* and end on *la* (the tonic or keynote is *la*). This approach stresses the relationship between the major and minor scales.

A natural minor scale   *A harmonic minor scale*

| do | re | me | fa | sol | le | te | do |
| la | ti | do | re | mi | fa | sol | la |

| do | re | me | fa | sol | le | ti | do |
| la | ti | do | re | mi | fa | si | la |

A melodic minor scale

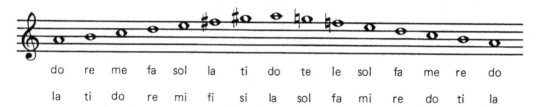

| do | re | me | fa | sol | la | ti | do | te | le | sol | fa | me | re | do |
| la | ti | do | re | mi | fi | si | la | sol | fa | mi | re | do | ti | la |

IDENTIFYING MINOR KEYS

Determine the minor key for the following pieces. Use the guidelines to help in this identification.

Guidelines for Identifying Minor Keys

Step 1. Examine the key signature to determine the major key possibility and the minor key possibility.

Step 2. To eliminate one possibility (from step 1), check the final pitch of the piece. Most often, that will be the tonic.

Step 3. If you think a minor tonic is indicated, check the melody to see if accidentals are used. (Remember that the harmonic and melodic minor scales will have accidentals added to the melody.) The results of steps 1 and 2 will identify the minor key.

Adagio

Daniel Gottlob Türk (Germany, 1750–1813)

English Carol

Jimmy Page (England, b. 1944)
Robert Plant (England, b. 1948)

Stairway to Heaven (excerpt)

There's a la - dy who's sure all that glit - ters is gold __ and she's

buy - ing a stair - way to heav - en, when she gets there she knows if the

stores all are closed with a word she can get what she came for.

Canon   Konrad Max Künz (Germany, 1812–1875)

HARMONY

PRIMARY CHORDS IN MINOR

To construct the primary chords in minor,* the harmonic minor scale usually serves as the framework. The i and the iv chords are always minor, and the V and the V7 chords are always major and major-minor sevenths (as in a major key).

Primary chords in A minor

i, iv$_4^6$, and V$_5^6$ Chords in Selected Minor Keys

As in major, the primary chords in minor can be rearranged or inverted for ease in moving from one chord to the next. The same inversions for the iv (second inversion) and the V7 (first inversion) are used in harmonic minor.

*i, iv, and V7 chords for minor keys are shown in Appendix G. RH and LH fingerings are also provided.

Key of A minor

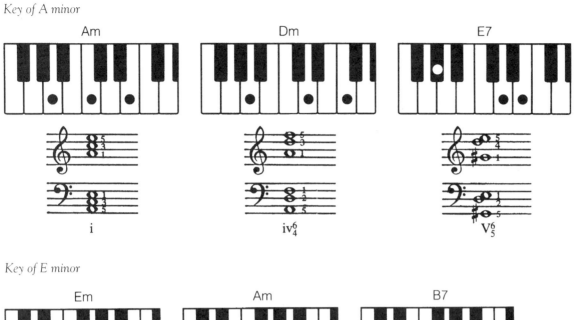

Key of E minor

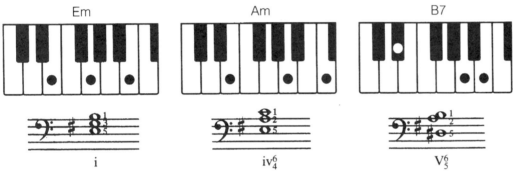

Key of B minor

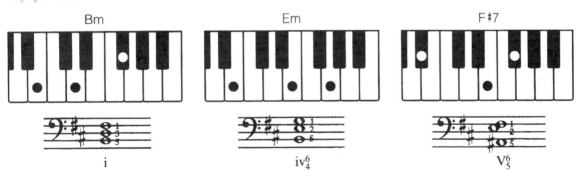

Key of D minor

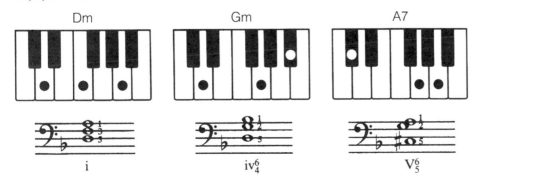

Key of G minor

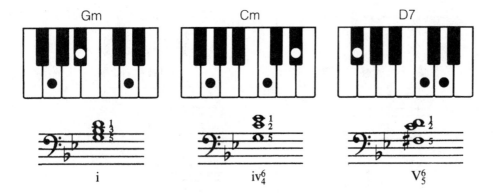

Key of C minor

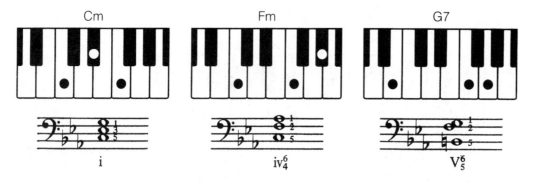

Key of F minor

Performing i–iv$^6_4$–V$^6_5$

1. Perform the following exercise to practice the moves between the three chords. When you move from i to iv$^6_4$, notice how the bottom notes of the two chords stay the same while the middle note moves up a whole step and the top note moves up a half step. When changing from the i to the V$^6_5$, the top note stays the same, the middle note moves up a whole step, and the bottom note moves down a half step. The fingerings and the whole-step–half-step

moves will be the same in any minor key. Memorize this progression. Learn to shift quickly and smoothly from one chord to another. Feel the shape of the next chord, and actually touch the keys just before playing. Transpose this exercise to other minor keys.

i–iv$_4^6$–V$_5^6$ Exercise

Part A

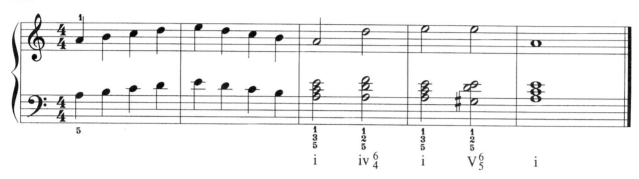

Part B

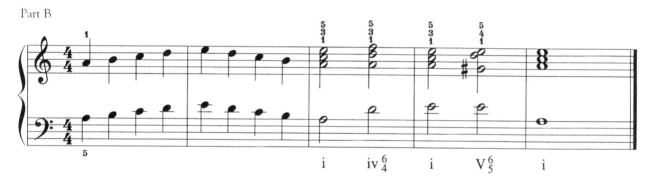

Part C

2. Use legato pedaling for the next exercise of the primary chords. Try not to blur chord tones or overlap sounds of single notes. Connect evenly when crossing hands. Transpose to other minor keys.

Arpeggio Exercise: i–iv$_4^6$–V$_5^6$

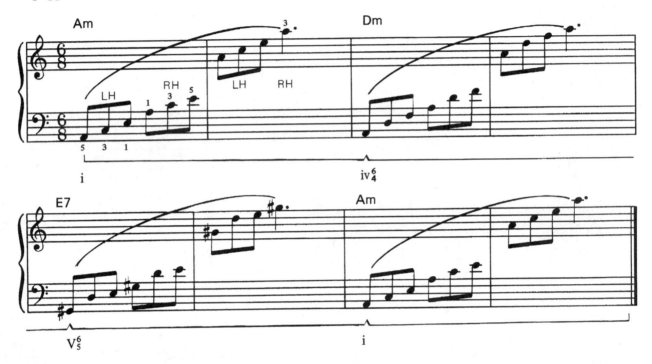

3. Perform the following pieces. Determine the minor key and the primary chords first; then practice the chord progression. Be sure to review the rhythm, form, and fingering for each piece before performing. Transpose to other minor keys.

Chording with i and V$_5^6$

Folk Melody 8

Folk Melody 9

Chording with i–iv$_4^6$–V$_5^6$

This Old Hammer

American Folk Melody

Czech Folk Melody 2

Joshua Fought the Battle of Jericho

Moderato   African-American Spiritual

Harmonizations with i, iv, and V7 Chords

Accompany the following melodies with the i, iv, and V7 chords. (Refer to guidelines on p. 165). Try different accompaniment patterns (broken chord and arpeggio), too.

Chording with i and V$^6_3$

Folk Melody 10

Hungarian Folk Melody 2

German Dance No. 1 (excerpt)

Franz Schubert (Austria, 1797–1828)

Chording with i–iv$_4^6$–V$_5^6$

Canterbury

English Folk Melody

Folk Melody 11

RELATIVE MAJORS AND MINORS

Major and minor scales sharing the same key signatures are *related* (see "Minor Key Signatures" earlier in this chapter). Often in compositions, especially long pieces, both the major and the relative minor (or vice versa) are used.

"We Three Kings of Orient Are" is in E minor in the A section and in G relative major in the B section. Practice one section at a time. Notice the $\frac{3}{8}$ time signature:

$$\left(\begin{array}{l} 3 = 3 \text{ beats in a measure} \\ 8 = \text{♪ receives one beat} \end{array} \right)$$

We Three Kings

John H. Hopkins (United States, mid-19th c.)

PARALLEL MAJORS AND MINORS

Just as major and minor scales and keys can have the same key signature but different tonics, so major and minor scales and keys can have the same tonic but different key signatures. When a major and a minor scale begin on the same tonic, they are said to be *parallel majors and minors*. For example, C major and C minor are **parallel keys.**

C major   *C minor*

"Ah, vous dirai-je, Maman" is presented here in its original scale (C major) and in the parallel minor. Play both versions.

Ah, vous dirai-je, Maman (C major)

Ah, vous dirai-je, Maman (C minor)

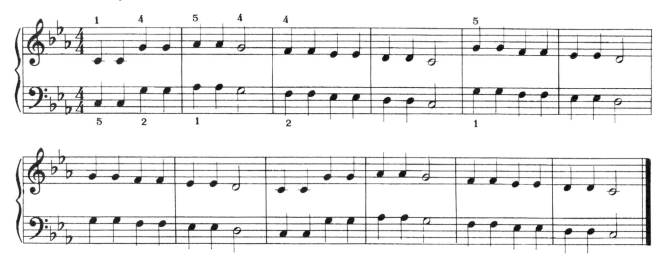

FORM

THEME AND VARIATIONS

Since the 1600s, keyboard players have performed compositions based on the form **theme and variations.** A theme and variations is a series of variations on a given melody. Although some theme and variations are improvised at the keyboard, many composers over the years have written a set of variations on a popular song or dance, a chorale tune, or a theme they or someone else composed.

Variations are created by altering the rhythm, the melody, or the harmony (or all three) of the **theme.** For example, the rhythm could be altered by changing the meter, or the melody could be varied by changing from major to minor or vice versa. If "Ah, vous dirai-je, Maman" were used as the theme for such a composition, one variation could include the change of mode from major to minor (as in the parallel minor example). Another variation could feature a change of meter from $\frac{4}{4}$ to $\frac{3}{4}$.

In 1778 Wolfgang Amadeus Mozart composed a set of variations on the theme "Ah, vous dirai-je, Maman." The theme follows in its entirety, but only excerpts of the twelve variations are included. Study this example and determine the melodic, rhythmic, and harmonic changes made for each variation. A live or recorded performance of Mozart's entire composition will help you to hear what you see and see what you hear.

12 Variations on "Ah, vous dirai-je, Maman," K. 265*

Theme   Wolfgang Amadeus Mozart (Austria, 1756–1791)

*The K used in W. Mozart's works is an abbreviation for Köchel. L. von Köchel chronologically catalogued Mozart's more than 600 compositions.

Var. I (excerpt)

Var. II (excerpt)

Var. III (excerpt)

Var. IV (excerpt)

Var. V (excerpt)

Var. VI (excerpt)

Var. VII (excerpt)

Var. VIII (excerpt)

Var. IX (excerpt)

Var. X (excerpt)

Var. XI (excerpt)

Adagio

Var. XII (excerpt)

Allegro

COMPOSING PROJECT

Theme and Variations

Create a theme-and-variations composition based on a familiar melody.

Step 1. Choose a familiar melody that you can play well. Some possibilities are "When the Saints Go Marching In," p. 72, "Love Somebody" (Piano 2), p. 282, "I Never Will Marry," p. 164, and "Kum Ba Yah," p. 167.

Step 2. Using the selected melody, create one variation that illustrates a change of mode (if your melody is in major, use the parallel minor, and if your melody is in minor, use the parallel major). Experiment, and when you have finalized your variation, notate it on the staff.

Step 3. Create a second variation on the original melody, illustrating a change of rhythm. You can either vary the rhythm of the melody or change the meter. Notate your variation.

Step 4. Play your Theme and Two Variations, reading from staff notation. Exchange your melody with a classmate's. Play your pieces for each other, and assess your work for accuracy and creativity.

ENSEMBLE PLAYING

Chapter 9 Ensemble Pieces:

1. "Shalom, Chaverim," pp. 300–301
2. "Zum Gali Gali," pp. 300–301
3. Scherzo from *Melodious Pieces*, pp. 302–303

REPERTOIRE

Notice the minor five-finger range for "Round Dance." What can you say about the pitches in the final measure?

Round Dance (from *First Term at the Piano*)

Andante moderato

Béla Bartók (Hungary, 1881–1945)

In this Kabalevsky piece, which interval is used almost exclusively? Notice the jump from the ascending interval to the descending one. First practice measures 1–3 separately very slowly, using the drop/lift technique (see Chapter 7). Then work on the entire piece.

Op. 39, No. 4 (from *24 Little Pieces*)

Dmitri Kabalevsky (Russia, 1904–1987)

What is the overall form of "Minuet"? Notice that the A section is in minor (which form?). The B section begins in relative major F but quickly moves back to D minor.

Minuet

Leopold Mozart (Austria, 1719–1787)

TECHNIQUE EXERCISES

Exercise 1: Extension Fingering and Interval Study   This exercise focuses on the intervals within the three minor scales. Notice the new intervals: the minor sixth (m6) and the minor seventh (m7). (Remember, minor intervals are always a half step smaller than major ones.) Feel the distance as you play, and listen to the sound of each. Practice hands separately and hands together. Transpose to other minor keys.

Natural minor

Harmonic minor

Melodic minor

Exercise 2: Contraction Fingering This exercise stresses contraction within the five-finger pattern. Fingers are actually brought closer together. Practice hands separately and hands together. Play without accidentals (in parentheses) for the major pattern and with accidentals for the minor pattern. Transpose to the parallel major and minors of G, F, D, A, E, and B.

Exercise 3: Technical Study After this study is secure as notated, change to
the C parallel minor (harmonic).

Study (from Op. 823)   Carl Czerny (Austria, 1791–1851)

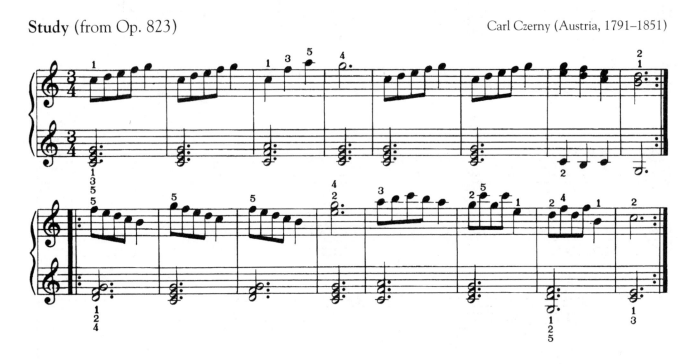

Exercise 4: Independent Use of Fingers In this exercise, the thumb and the
little finger play the whole notes while the other fingers play the quarter notes.
Practice hands separately first, then hands together. Change to the parallel minor;
then transpose to other major and minor patterns.

Part A

Part B

CHAPTER EVALUATION

1. Play the pitches in the natural, harmonic, and melodic minor scales on the following tonics: D, G, E, and C.

2. Perform the G harmonic minor scale in two octaves ascending and descending.

3. Play the i, iv⁶, V⁶ chords in the following minor keys (harmonic form): A, E, B, D, and G.

4. Demonstrate parallel majors and minors by choosing a major melody to play. Perform the melody in major and in the parallel minor.

5. Perform the following melody accurately and musically. Be able to describe the melodic and rhythmic characteristics and its overall design. Transpose the melody to the key of D minor. Harmonize with i and V7 chords.

Bim Bom

Israeli Folk Melody

6. Write the specified minor scales.

7. Notate the minor tonics for the following key signatures.

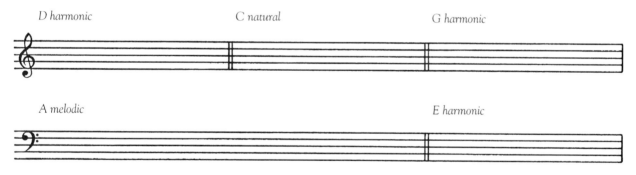

8. Write the primary chords for the stated key in root position and then in the i-iv$_4^6$-V$_3^6$ position.

E minor

         i   iv   V7   i   i   iv$_4^6$ V$_5^6$ i

G minor

         i   iv   V7   i   i   iv$_4^6$ V$_5^6$ i

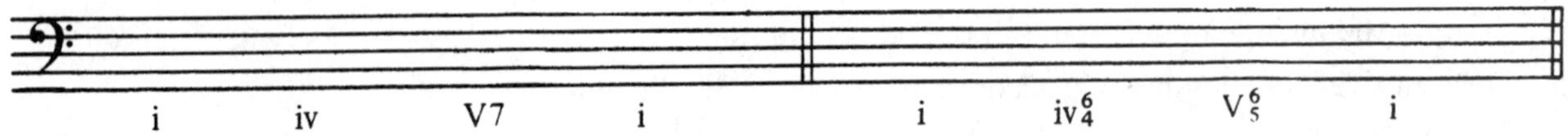

9. Describe the following musical terms:

     a. Natural minor

     b. Harmonic minor

     c. Melodic minor

     d. Relative majors and minors

     e. Parallel majors and minors

     f. Contraction fingering

     g. Theme and variations

10. Identify the following musical symbols:

     a. i   iv$_4^6$ V$_3^6$

     b. $\frac{3}{8}$

     c. Bm

     d. E7

10

MELODY

PENTATONIC SCALES

Although major and minor scales have been widely used in the music of Western civilization and are certainly the most familiar to us, other scales and modes have been used and are still being used today. Of all the scales, the **pentatonic scale** (*penta* means five) may be the oldest. This five-tone scale serves as the basis for much of world music, particularly music of Northeast Asia, Native America, Africa, and Europe, and it often forms the basis of ostinati in rock music. Pentatonic melodies are also found in the works of Western art music composers, for example, Debussy's "Voiles."

The pentatonic scale most frequently used includes no half steps and one interval of a whole step plus a half step. This familiar pentatonic scale can be illustrated on the five black keys and transposed to the white keys.

Pentatonic scale

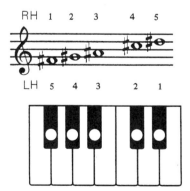

Pentatonic scale

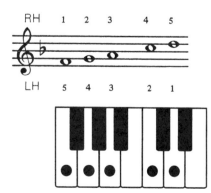

Major and minor key signatures are adapted for pentatonic music by choosing the signature that results in the five necessary pitches. The key signature will not always identify the tonic as it does for major and minor scales. Because there is no leading tone in the pentatonic scale, some pentatonic music does not have an obvious tonic.

Performing Pentatonic Melodies

1. Play the preceding pentatonic scale on the black keys, and then transpose to the white keys.

2. Perform "Taiwan School Song" as written, then on the black keys by thinking of each note as being sharped.

Taiwan School Song

Yang wa____ wa   Syan syi____ syi   Yu le yi ge   yang wa____ wa.

Ni tsung na li lai,   Ni wang na li chu.   Yu le yi ge   yang wa____ wa.

© 1981, Patricia Hackett. Useed by permission. (*The Melody Book*, 2nd ed. Englewood Cliffs, N.J.: Prentice-Hall, Inc., 1991.)

3. Perform "Sakura," which uses a pentatonic scale that includes half steps (E F A B C). Notice the drone accompaniment.

Sakura   Japanese Folk Melody

4. Perform other pentatonic melodies in *PianoLab:*

   "Tom Dooley," p. 159

   "Amazing Grace," p. 271

   "Kang Ding City," p. 262

   "Auld Lang Syne," p. 265

5. Improvise with the pentatonic scale by playing only on black keys. Review "Improvisation—Black Keys," in Chapter 1.

MODES

Modes (seven-tone scales) served as the basis of most Western music through the seventeenth century. Between 1700 and 1900 the modes, from which our major and minor scales emerged, were seldom used. However, nineteenth- and twentieth-century composers rediscovered modal scales. Modes are used today in classical music, jazz, and popular music. Often, contemporary composers mix modes and scales within a piece.

Basically, the modes, also referred to as *church modes,* are seven-tone scales that include five whole steps and two half steps. Together with major and minor scales, they can be illustrated on the white keys of the piano.

As with minor scales, two approaches are used for associating syllables with modes.

1. The mode begins with *do*. The remaining syllables are altered when necessary.

2. The keynote is *do*. Each mode begins with the syllable name that pitch would have in the major scale of that key. This approach stresses the relationship of the modes to the tonic of the major scale (Dorian is up a major second, Phrygian is up a major third, and so on).

Modes and Scales

Major scale

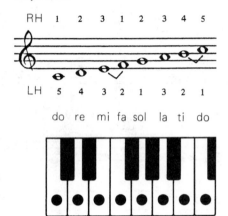

```
RH   1   2   3   1   2   3   4   5
LH   5   4   3   2   1   3   2   1
     do  re  mi  fa  sol la  ti  do
```

Dorian mode (natural minor with raised 6th)

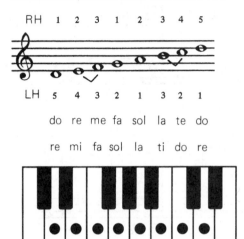

```
RH   1   2   3   1   2   3   4   5
LH   5   4   3   2   1   3   2   1
     do  re  me  fa  sol la  te  do
     re  mi  fa  sol la  ti  do  re
```

Phrygian mode (natural minor with lowered 2nd)

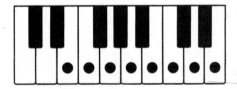

```
RH   1   2   3   1   2   3   4   5
LH   5   4   3   2   1   3   2   1
     do  ra  me  fa  sol le  te  do
     mi  fa  sol la  ti  do  re  mi
```

Lydian mode (major with raised 4th)

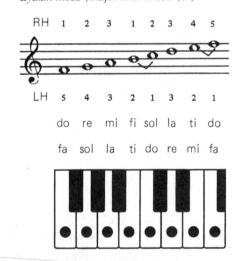

```
RH   1   2   3   1   2   3   4   5
LH   5   4   3   2   1   3   2   1
     do  re  mi  fi  sol la  ti  do
     fa  sol la  ti  do  re  mi  fa
```

Mixolydian mode (major with lowered 7th)

```
RH   1   2   3   1   2   3   4   5
LH   5   4   3   2   1   3   2   1
     do  re  mi  fa  sol la  te  do
     sol la  ti  do  re  mi  fa  sol
```

Minor scale (natural)

```
RH   1   2   3   1   2   3   4   5
LH   5   4   3   2   1   3   2   1
     do  re  me  fa  sol le  te  do
```

Locrian mode (seldom used)

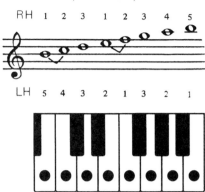

The modes may be transposed to any pitch, but because of the variety of whole-step–half-step formulas, they may be more difficult to recognize in transposed form. Often major and minor key signatures are adapted for transposed modal music. The Dorian and Mixolydian modes are especially popular with composers of jazz and commercial music. (Much of the Beatles' music is modal, frequently mixing modes and major and minor within a piece.)

Performing the Modes

1. Practice each of the preceding modes, listening for the special qualities of each. The fingering is indicated above and below the notes.

2. Choose a mode and improvise a bit at the keyboard with the pitches in that mode. Move freely between left and right hands. Experiment until you come up with something that pleases you.

3. Perform the following two pieces. Determine which mode each is based on (both are in original form, not transposed form).

Scarborough Fair   English Folk Song

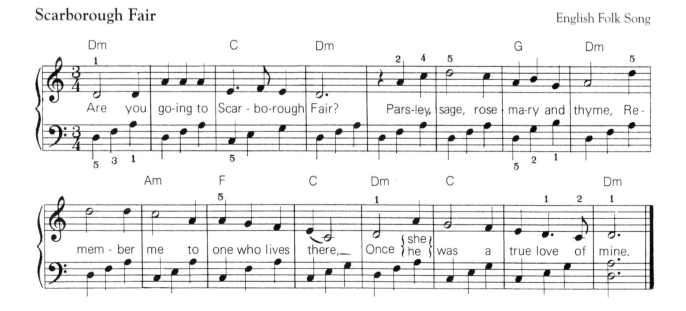

The Great Silke   Scottish Folk Melody

THE WHOLE-TONE SCALE

Scales using equidistant tones are common in Southeast Asia and enjoyed a brief vogue in early twentieth-century Europe, especially in the music of the French Impressionist composers Debussy and Ravel. The **whole-tone scale,** a six-tone scale, consists solely of whole steps. The two forms of the whole-tone scale are shown here.

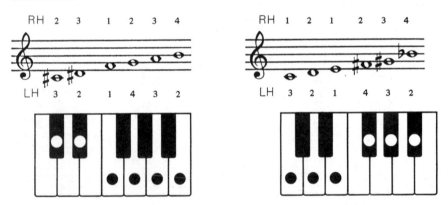

As used by the Impressionist composers, this scale lacks a feeling of tonic and conveys ambiguity, a sense of vagueness, a musically indefinite quality (an impression). Since no major or minor key signature can be used for whole-tone music, accidentals are included in the music.

Performing Whole-Tone Scales

1. Improvise on the whole-tone scale with the damper pedal depressed. Freely move between the low, middle, and high registers of the piano. Use arpeggio figures. Be experimental with rhythms.

2. Identify the whole-tone scale in Vladimir Rebikov's composition. What accompaniment figure is used in the LH?

The Bear

Andante

Vladimir Rebikov (Russia, 1886–1920)

THE BLUES SCALE

The special form of jazz called the blues uses a **blues scale.** This scale can only be approximated in traditional notation or on the keyboard because the "blue notes" fall somewhere between the pitches and keys we know. To approximate the pitches in a blues scale, take the traditional major scale and flat the third and the seventh pitches (the fifth is also flatted in some of the music of the bebop era).

Blues scale

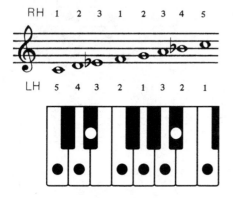

Performing the Blues Scale

1. Play the blues scale in C (as in the preceding example) hands separately. Experiment with rhythmic variations as you get familiar with the sound of the scale. Transpose the blues scale to F major and to G major.

2. Perform "Emily's Blues." Notice how the C, the F, and the G blues scales are all included.

Emily's Blues

Diana Somers

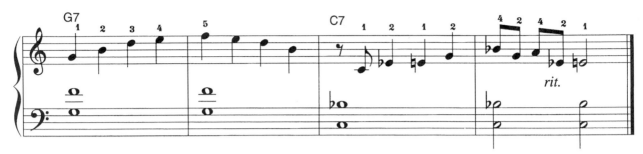

© 1991, Diana Somers. Used by permission.

Diana Somers composed this blues composition while a student in a beginning piano and music fundamentals class at San Francisco State University.

3. Play the ensemble piece "Razzle Dazzle" by Lee Evans on pp. 306–307. This piece is based on the blues scale.

BITONALITY

Twentieth-century composers have explored the use of two or more **tonalities** (or keys) occurring simultaneously. When two tonalities are performed at the same time, the result is **bitonality.**

Performing Bitonal Music

1. Perform Bartók's "Dialogue," which may be considered bitonal. The RH part is within the A minor five-finger pattern, and the LH part is within the E major pattern. Practice the parts separately and together.

Dialogue (from *First Term at the Piano*)

Moderato

Béla Bartók (Hungary, 1881–1945)

2. Improvise with bitonality. Use a different major or minor five-finger pattern in each hand. Be flexible with rhythm. Explore various registers of the piano and the use of pedal.

ATONALITY

Twentieth-century composers have also experimented with pitch organizations that suggest no tonality or key. Music in which all pitches have an equal function and no one tone serves as the tonic is referred to as **atonal.**

Tone Rows

One atonal pitch organization involves arranging the twelve pitches of the chromatic scale (a twelve-tone scale consisting entirely of half steps) into a series (**serial music**), or a **twelve-tone row.** Thousands of rows can be formed from the chromatic scale. The series is then used without alteration according to the following rules.

1. O—**Original:** Row is played exactly in the planned order, one note after the other.

2. R—**Retrograde:** Row is played backwards, one note after the other.

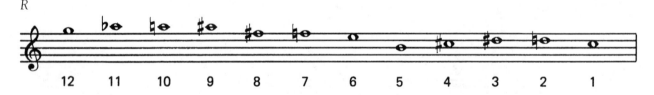

3. I—**Inversion:** Row is played with the same intervals of the original, but with each interval inverted (upside down or in "mirror" version).

4. RI—**Retrograde Inversion:** Row is played in inverted form in retrograde (backwards and upside down).

R-I

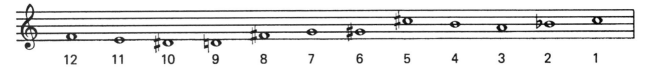

Performing Tone Rows

1. Perform the original form of the tone row in any rhythm you choose or without any rhythm at all. Use both hands to play each note in any register you wish. Follow this rule: Once you have used a tone in the row, do not reuse it until the other eleven tones have been used.

2. Perform all four forms of the tone row.

3. Discover which forms of the preceding tone row are used in "Two-Handed Duet." Remember that any octave position and enharmonic spelling of the pitches are possible, and any clef, range, simultaneous playing of tones, and repetition of tones may be used. Notice how the rhythm ties the composition together.

Two-Handed Duet (X from *32 Piano Games*)

♩ = 160

Ross Lee Finney (United States, b. 1906)

R H Y T H M

SHIFTING METER

A rhythmic effect of irregularity can be achieved by **shifting meters.** Shifting meter occurs when there are meter changes throughout a composition—for example, $\frac{3}{4}$ to $\frac{4}{4}$ to $\frac{3}{4}$. To indicate shifting meters, a new meter signature is written within each measure where the meter changes.

Rhythm Exercise: Shifting Meter Clap, count, or play on any key(s) the following examples of shifting meters.

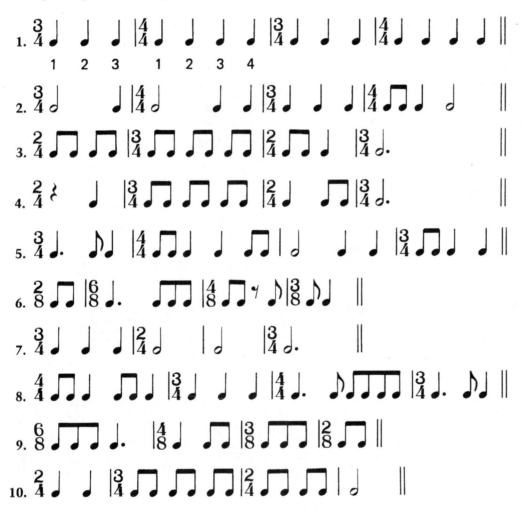

Performing Shifting Meter

Stravinsky's "Andantino" shifts from $\frac{2}{4}$ to $\frac{3}{4}$ to $\frac{2}{4}$ at the end of the first section. Clap and count the rhythm before playing. Notice that both hands stay within the five-finger position; note the A B A form of the piece.

Andantino (No. 1 from *The Five Fingers*) Igor Stravinsky (Russia, 1882–1971)

ASYMMETRIC METER

Asymmetric meter occurs when the accents within a measure are spaced irregularly. This gives an effect of constant shifting of accents throughout an entire piece and is often heard in Eastern European and Greek music and in twentieth-century music.

Asymmetric meters

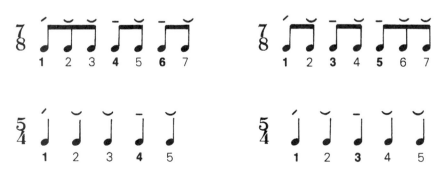

Performing Asymmetric Meters

1. Perform "Yugoslavian Folk Melody" in ⅞, observing that the accents occur on beats 1 and 5. Clap the rhythm of the RH part before playing.

Yugoslavian Folk Melody

2. Clap the rhythm of this excerpt from Dave Brubeck's "Blue Rondo a la Turk." In the first three measures, the accents occur on beats 1, 3, 5, and 7 of the ⁹⁄₈ meter, and in the last measure, the accents occur on beats 1, 4, and 7. Perform when the rhythm is secure.

Blue Rondo a la Turk (excerpt)   Dave Brubeck (United States, b. 1920)

Copyright © 1960, Derry Music Company, San Francisco, California. Used by permission.

3. "Clusterphobia" includes shifting meter (⁵⁄₄ to ³⁄₄), asymmetric meter (⁵⁄₄), and no meter (0). The five-note clusters are to be performed entirely on white keys with fingers 1-2-3-4-5 in both hands. Both damper and soft pedals remain down throughout.

Clusterphobia

Very slowly   Nancy Van de Vate (United States, b. 1930)

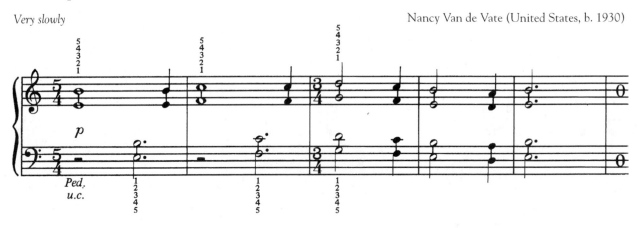

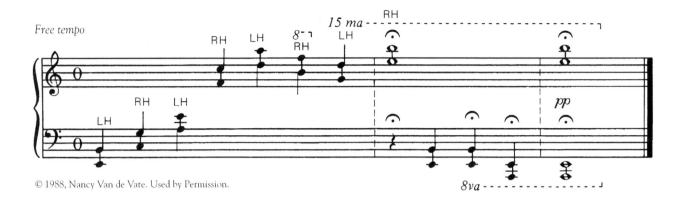

© 1988, Nancy Van de Vate. Used by Permission.

COMPOSING PROJECT

Twelve-Tone Row Composition

Create a composition based on a twelve-tone row.

Step 1. Decide on your tone row by arranging the twelve pitches of the chromatic scale in a specific order. (See the example on p. 220). This arrangement will serve as your original form.

Step 2. Experiment with this original form, using any rhythm you choose. Distribute the row between the LH and the RH. When you have finalized your rhythm and your keyboard position, notate.

Step 3. Continue your composition by manipulating the row in original and retrograde forms (see the example on p. 220) as many times as you wish to complete the piece. Also, consider incorporating varying dynamics, tempo, and shifting meters. Notate your composition.

Step 4. Play your Twelve-Tone Row composition, reading from staff notation. Exchange your melody with a classmate's. Play your pieces for each other, and assess your work for accuracy and creativity.

ENSEMBLE PLAYING

Chapter 10 Ensemble Pieces:

1. "Every Night When the Sun Goes In," pp. 304–305
2. "Razzle Dazzle," pp. 306–307
3. "Calico Rag," pp. 308–309

REPERTOIRE

"Joy" stays within the D-to-A range in both hands. Notice the two measures that include chromatic tones in the RH. As you practice hands together, observe the **imitation** between lines. What is the form of this piece?

Joy

Allegretto   Cornelius Gurlitt (Germany, 1820–1901)

Visually analyze Op. 39, No. 8, for key or mode identification, phrase structure, interval movement, fingerings, and rhythm. Play legato, paying careful attention to slurs.

Op. 39, No. 8 (from *24 Little Pieces*)

Andante   Dmitri Kabalevsky (Russia, 1904–1987)

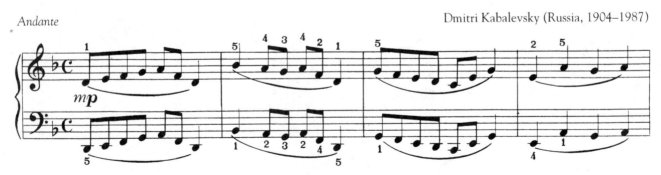

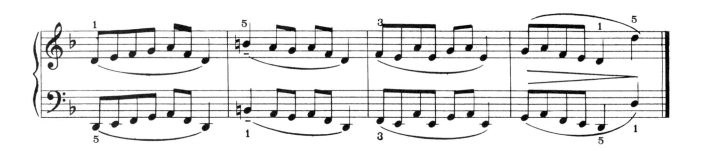

The interval of a major sixth (nine half steps) is featured in this **etude.** Only fingers 1 and 5 are used. Practice the major sixths alone first, then the entire piece.

Etude No. 9

Very fast ($\d = 112$)

John Biggs (United States, b. 1932)

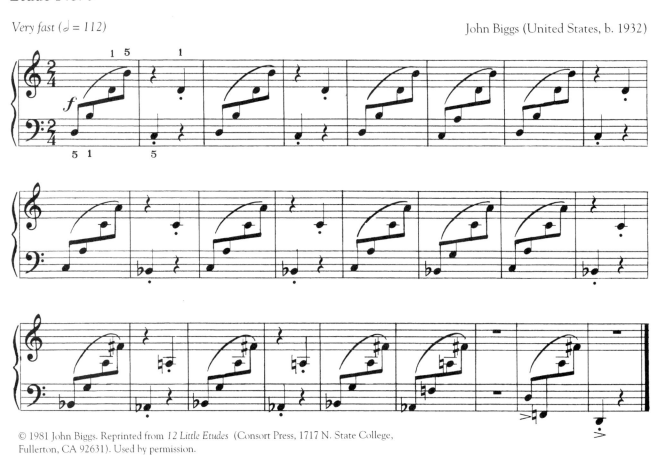

Leopold Mozart's "Minuet" is an example of A B, or binary, form. Notice how each section is repeated, and discover what part of A is repeated in B. Practice one section at a time.

From *Nannerl Notenbuch* (1759)

Minuet   Leopold Mozart (Austria, 1719–1787)

This minuet is one of the keyboard pieces included in the music book compiled by Leopold Mozart for his eight-year-old daughter, Nannerl. As a child, Nannerl concertized throughout Europe with her younger brother, Wolfgang Mozart, and won praise for her extraordinary keyboard skills.

TECHNIQUE EXERCISES

Exercise 1: Extension Fingering This exercise extends beyond the five-finger range and works on the third, fourth, and fifth fingers of the LH ascending, and the third, fourth, and fifth fingers of the RH descending. At first, practice very slowly, lifting fingers high and playing each note distinctly and evenly (hands together and then hands separately). Gradually increase the speed. Play legato.

The Virtuoso Pianist, No. 4 (simplified version)   Charles Louis Hanon (France, 1820–1900)

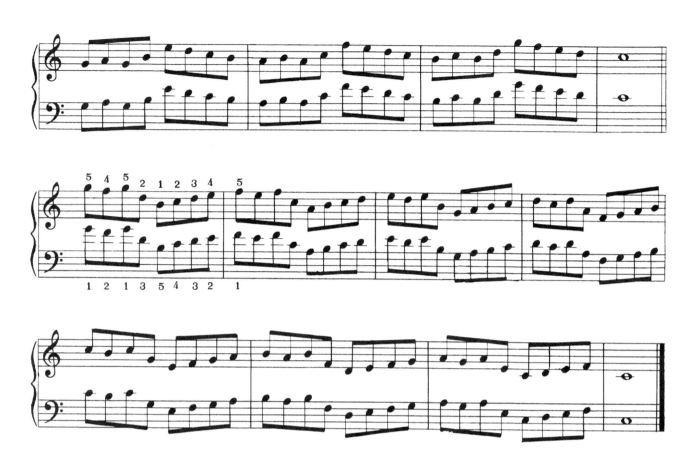

Exercise 2: Changing Fingers Practice this exercise with each hand separately. Change fingers while holding down the half notes. Also play the exercise changing between the following fingers:

RH: 3–2, 4–3, 5–4

LH: 2–3, 3–4, 4–5

Part A

Part B

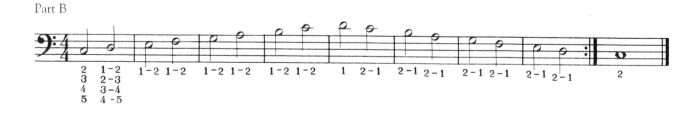

Exercise 3: Independent Use of Fingers In this exercise, the thumb and the little finger sustain notes, while the other fingers move independently. Practice with each hand alone and then hands together. Transpose to other major and minor patterns.

Part A

Part B

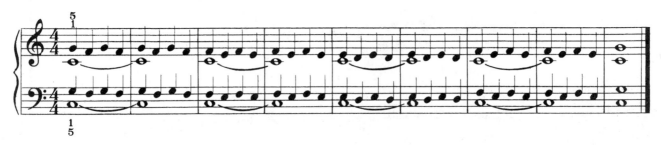

Exercise 4: Legato or Syncopated Pedaling Practice this Schumann piece slowly, using the legato or syncopated pedaling. Practice hands separately and then hands together.

Ein Choral
(from *Piano Pieces for the Young*, Op. 68)   Robert Schumann (Germany, 1810–1856)

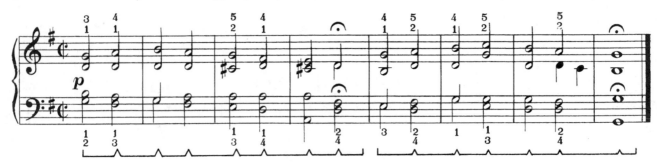

CHAPTER EVALUATION

1. At the keyboard, demonstrate a pentatonic scale, the Dorian mode, the Mixolydian mode, and a whole-tone scale.

2. Demonstrate changing fingers on the same key by playing Technique Exercise 2 in this chapter.

3. Play the bitonal piece "Dialogue" (Bartók), p. 219, with pitch and rhythmic accuracy. Be able to identify the two scales used.

4. Perform the twelve-tone row compositon "Two-Handed Duet," p. 221 with pitch and rhythmic accuracy. Be prepared to discuss the tone row and its manipulation in this piece.

5. Clap several examples of shifting meter in the rhythm exercise in this chapter.

6. Demonstrate legato pedaling by performing Schumann's "Ein Choral" (Technique Exercise 4).

7. Write the pitches in the pentatonic scale based on the following whole-step–half-step arrangement.

    A ____ ____ ____ ____ ____
       W   W   W&H   W

8. Notate the pitches in the designated modes on the staff and on the keyboard chart.

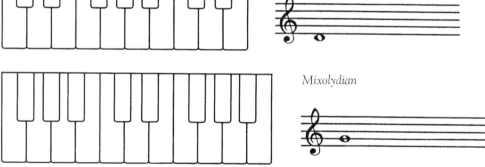

Dorian

Mixolydian

9. The following excerpt from a Chopin mazurka uses the pitches B♭ C D E F G A B♭. Determine on which mode this excerpt is based.

    _____

    (mode)

Mazurka in F Major, Op. 68, No. 3 (excerpt)

Poco più vivo   Frédéric Chopin (Poland, 1810–1849)

10. Write whole-tone scales on the given pitches.

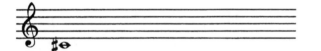 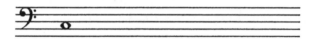

11. Create a twelve-tone row, and notate the row on the following staff.

12. One way to manipulate a tone row is to play it backwards or in _____ _____ form.

13. Notate four measures of a rhythm in any asymmetric meter of your choice.

14. Describe the following musical terms:

   a. Pentatonic scale

   b. Modes

   c. Whole-tone scale

   d. Blues scale

   e. Bitonality

   f. Atonality

   g. Tone row

   h. Shifting meter

   i. Asymmetric meter

15. Identify the following musical symbols:

   a.

   b.

   c.

SUPPLEMENTARY MUSIC

SUPPLEMENTARY CLASSICAL PIANO LITERATURE

What is the finger pattern for the LH and the RH in this piece? Observe the RH rests and staccato markings. Is the LH part similar to a particular accompaniment pattern?

Folk Song (No. 7 from *First Term at the Piano*)

Moderato   Béla Bartók (Hungary, 1881–1945)

"Little Rondo" includes only an A and a B section. Work on the A section of
this **rondo** (the LH part is a good technical exercise). What is different about
measures 9–16? When the A section is secure, continue to the B.

Little Rondo

Daniel Gottlob Türk (Germany, 1750–1813)

Determine the key and the primary chords for this **bagatelle.** For section B,
write the roman numeral identification for the chords in each measure.

Bagatelle

Moderato

Anton Diabelli (Austria, 1781–1858)

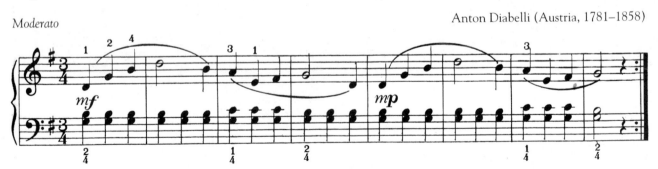

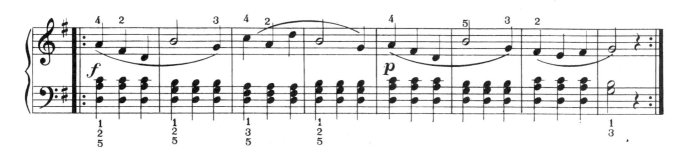

Minuets and other short pieces written in the eighteenth century are in two-part form (A B). Mozart's Minuet in G is a good example of binary form. Notice how easy it is to divide the melody into two-measure and four-measure groupings. How many measures are in each section? Practice one section at a time.

Minuet in G, K. 1

Wolfgang Amadeus Mozart (Austria, 1756–1791)

A child prodigy, Mozart wrote this minuet in 1761 or 1762 in Salzburg, Austria. The trio, a part of this minuet, is omitted in the preceding example.

---

* 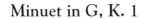 is a triplet (three notes of equal value within a beat that normally divides into twos: ♫).

Perform this eighteenth-century minuet in a moderate tempo and in the normal touch (*non legato*) of the period.

From *Notenbuch für Wolfgang* (1762)
Carl Philipp Emanuel Bach (Germany, 1714–1788)

Minuet

"Schwaebisch" (rustic dance) follows the eighteenth-century two-part form. Break down each section into smaller parts. How many measures seem to group together?

Johann Christoph Friedrich Bach
(Germany, 1732–1795)

Schwaebisch

Since "Growing" has no meter signature, what can you determine about the meter? Which note gets the beat?

Growing

Moderately slow

Emma Lou Diemer (United States, b. 1927)

What is the sectional form for Rameau's "Minuet"?

Minuet

Allegretto

Jean Philippe Rameau (France, 1683–1764)

Identify the key in which "March" begins and ends. What happens in the middle section?

March (from *Six Children's Pieces*)

Tempo di marcia

Dmitri Shostakovich (Russia, 1906–1975)

Notice the parallel motion between hands in the opening measures of the
Haydn composition. What is the same in the A and B sections?

German Dance, No. 2

Franz Joseph Haydn (Austria, 1732–1809)

Statement (from *Little Piano Book*, Op. 60)

Allegro (il ritmo sempre molto preciso)

Vincent Persichetti (United States, 1915–1987)

Decide whether "Bourrée" is in the major mode or the minor mode. Notice the short upbeat, one of the characteristics of a **bourrée.**

Bourrée

From *Notenbuch für Wolfgang* (1762)
Leopold Mozart (Austria, 1719–1787)

This excerpt from the popular "Für Elise" is in A minor. In what section is there a momentary shift to the relative major? Notice the importance of the arpeggio figure in this piece.

Für Elise (excerpt)

Poco moto   Ludwig van Beethoven (Germany, 1770–1827)

What is the sectional form for this minuet? Identify the rhythmic motive that is used.

Minuet in F, K. 2

Wolfgang Amadeus Mozart (Austria, 1756–1791)

Note the clef used for both the RH and the LH parts in Op. 39, No. 5. Pay close attention to the staccato and accent marks. Play slowly at first (hands together); then gradually increase your speed.

Op. 39, No. 5 (from *24 Little Pieces*)

Dmitri Kabalevsky (Russia, 1904–1987)

Lively

Consider eighteenth-century performance practices before playing this piece.
The touch would most likely be *non legato;* the tempo, *moderato;* and the dynamic
level, *mezzo forte.*

From *Notenbüchlein für Anna Magdalena Bach* (1725)
Johann Sebastian Bach (Germany, 1685–1750)

Minuet in G

Notice the compound meter, the LH accompaniment figure, and the grace notes ( ). Although the grace notes are to be performed quickly, they do not receive any specific time value.

Theme from 6 Variations on "Nel cor più non mi sento"

Andantino

Ludwig van Beethoven (Germany, 1770–1827)

Piano variations were very popular with composers of the **Classic period.** Beethoven wrote over twenty separate sets of piano variations on original or borrowed themes. "Nel cor più non mi sento" ("Why Feels My Heart So Dormant") is a borrowed theme from an aria by Giovanni Paisiello.

What is the form for this contemporary piece? Which keys or modes predominate? Observe the tempo, dynamic, and articulation markings.

Pastorale

Herbert Bielawa (United States, b. 1930)

Make the melody line "sing." Pay careful attention to phrasing. Notice that the LH part is notated in the treble clef and uses the same accompaniment figure throughout.

Stückchen (from *Piano Pieces for the Young*, Op. 68)

Nicht schnell

Robert Schumann (Germany, 1810–1856)

Does the A section end on the I or on the V? What about the B section? Notice the imitation at times between the RH and the LH. Consider eighteenth-century performance practices in regard to touch, dynamics, and tempo.

Minuet

Wilhelm Friedemann Bach (Germany, 1710–1784)

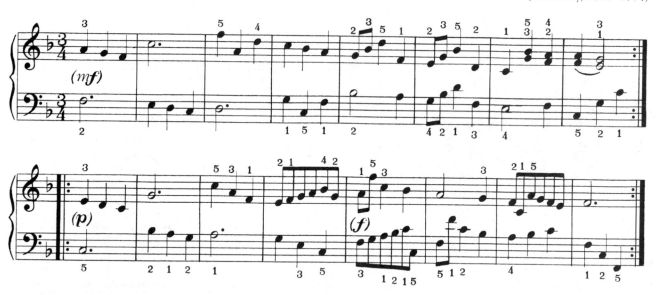

The Bartók composition, instead of being built on the all-white-key Dorian mode (D to D), is transposed to A. Before performing the piece, study the phrase structure to see where repeats occur.

III (from *For Children*)

Andante

Béla Bartók (Hungary, 1881–1945)

What kind of triads are used in both hands for the first and last four measures of "Prologue"? Pay close attention to the dynamic and tempo markings throughout the piece.

Prologue (from *Little Piano Book*, Op. 60)

Adagio pesante

Vincent Persichetti (United States, 1915–1987)

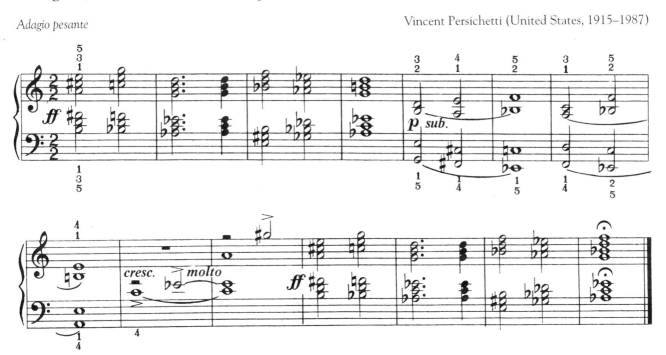

The sectional form for this mazurka is ____ ____ ____ . At the end of section B, notice the rolled chords (chord tones quickly "rolled" from bottom note to top; ⸁ = rolled chord).

Mazurka No. 3 (from *24 Mazurkas*)

Maria Szymanowska (Poland, 1789–1831)

Note the shifting meters in "Shifting Shadows." How many sections does the composition divide into? Are there any similarities between sections?

Shifting Shadows

Slowly (♪ = 108–116)

Nancy Van de Vate (United States, b. 1930)

Slightly faster (♪ = 63)

Prelude, Op. 28, No. 4

Largo   Frédéric Chopin (Poland, 1810–1849)

SUPPLEMENTARY BLUES, BOOGIE, AND RAGTIME

Analyze the first eight bars of "No Name Blues" and decide if the harmonies are predominantly triads or seventh chords. What rhythmic effect is achieved by eighth rests on the first beats of measures?

No Name Blues

Theresa McGlone

Theresa McGlone composed this piece while enrolled in a beginning piano and music fundamentals course at San Francisco State University.

Notice the rhythmic variety created by the triplet in this blues piece. Why is the grace note important?

Blue, Blue, Blue

Matt Zlatunich

© 1980, Matt Zlatunich. Used by permission.

Matt Zlatunich composed this blues composition while a student in a beginning piano and music fundamentals class at San Francisco State University.

The seventh chord (major-minor seventh) is featured throughout this "boogie." Circle and label the nonchord tones in the LH part.

Walkin' Boogie

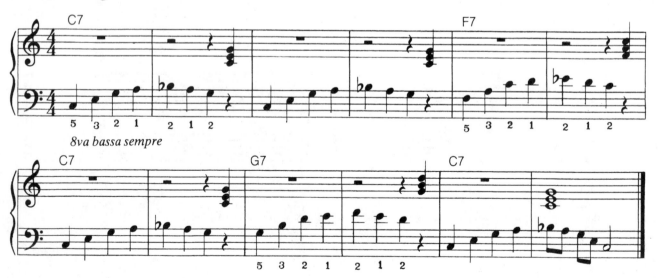

Keep your LH walking bass steady as you feel the beat groupings of 4 in this
compound meter piece.

Slow-Walkin' Guy

With a steady, relaxed swing

Tony Caramia

"The Entertainer" of 1902 played an important role in the ragtime revival of the 1970s when the rag, **ragtime,** and Joplin himself were popularized by the hit movie *The Sting*. Notice the syncopated melody line (accents on offbeats) in "The Entertainer." Practice the characteristic jump bass (stride bass)* in the LH. Refer to the chord sheet in Appendix I for explanation of chord symbols used in this rag.

The Entertainer (A Ragtime Two-Step)
(Sections A and B simplified)

Not too fast   Scott Joplin (United States, 1868–1917)

Create a jump bass accompaniment (easy stride or full stride) for "Red Rambler Rag." Refer to the patterns in Appendix H, 8a or 8b, and the notated accompaniment in "The Entertainer."

Red Rambler Rag

Julia Lee Niebergall (United States, 1886–1968)

*See Appendix H, 8a and 8b, for other stride bass patterns.

SUPPLEMENTARY SONGS WITH ACCOMPANIMENTS

He's Got the Whole World in His Hands

African-American Spiritual

He's got the whole world— in his hands,—He's got the whole world—
in his hands,He's got the whole world in his hands,He's got the whole world in his hands.

Kang Ding City

Chinese Folk Song

Pau ma lyou, lyou de shan shang, Yi dwo lyou, lyou de yun, Ah! Dwan, dwan lyou, lyou de jau_dzai,

Kang Ding lyou, lyou de cheng, Ah! Ywe lyang, wan, wan,___ Kang Ding lyou, lyou de cheng, Ah!

Silent Night

Joseph Mohr (Austria, 1792–1848)
Franz Gruber (Austria, 1789–1863)

Si - lent night, ho - ly night. All is calm, all is bright,

Round yon vir - gin moth-er and child, Ho - ly in-fant so ten - der and mild,

Sleep in heav-en-ly peace,___ Sleep_ in heav-en-ly peace.

With a Little Help from My Friends
(excerpt—rhythmically simplified)

John Lennon (England, 1940–1980)
Paul McCartney (England, b. 1942)

1. What would you do if I sang out of tune, would you stand up and walk out on
2. Lend me your ears and I'll sing you a song and I'll try not to sing out of

me? key. Oh, I get by with a lit-tle help from my friends.

Sinkiang Folk Dance

Chinese Folk Dance

© 1981, Patricia Hackett. Used by permission. (*The Melody Book*, 2nd ed. Englewood Cliffs, N.J.: Prentice-Hall, 1991.)

Hymne (excerpt)

Slowly   Vangelis Papathanassiau (Greece, 20th c.)

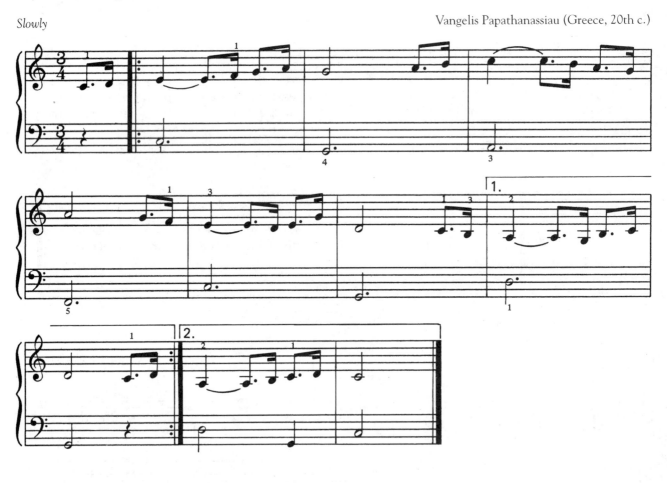

It Don't Mean a Thing
if It Ain't Got That Swing (excerpt)

"Duke" Ellington (United States, 1899–1974)
Arranged by Dee Spencer

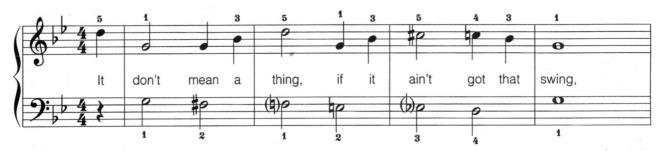

It don't mean a thing, if it ain't got that swing,

(doo wah, — doo wah,   doo wah, — doo wah,   doo wah, — doo wah,   doo wah, doo wah

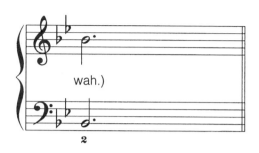

Auld Lang Syne

Scottish Folk Song

Give My Regards to Broadway

George M. Cohan (United States, 1878–1942)

Give my re- gards to Broad - way. Re - mem-ber me to Her - ald Square. Tell all the gang at For - ty - sec-ond St. that I will soon be there. Whis-per of how I'm yearn - ing to min-gle with the old time throng; Give my re- gards to old Broad - way and say that I'll be there, ere long.

We Shall Overcome

American Freedom Melody

We shall o-ver-come,— we shall o-ver-come,— we shall o-ver-come some day— — oh,— deep in my heart I do be-lieve that we shall o-ver-come some day.

Katherine Lee Bates (United States, 1859–1929)
Samuel A. Ward (United States, 1847–1903)
Arranged by Alexander Post

America, the Beautiful

O beau-ti-ful for spa-cious skies, For am-ber waves of grain, For pur-ple moun-tain maj-es-ties, A-bove the fruit-ed plain! A-mer-i-ca! A-mer-i-ca! God shed His grace on thee, And crown thy good with broth-er-hood From sea to shin-ing sea!

Words by Eleanor Farjeon
Gaelic Melody

Morning Has Broken

Samuel F. Smith (United States, 1808–1895)
Henry Carey (England, 1685–1743)
Arranged by Alexander Post

America

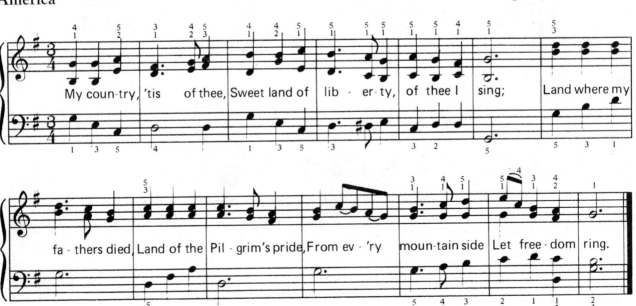

Memory from *Cats* (excerpt—rhythmically simplified)

Trevor Nunn, after T. S. Eliot
Andrew Lloyd Webber (England, b. 1948)

SUPPLEMENTARY SONGS (MELODIES ONLY)

The following melodies do not have LH accompaniments notated. Rather, suggested chords (by letter-name symbols) appear above each melody. These symbols should serve as a guide for creating your own accompaniments. Refer to Appendix I for explanations of unfamiliar chord symbols.

Since the symbols indicate only the letter name and the chord quality, you may choose to use the root of the chord alone, any chord tone, the entire chord in root position, or the chord in one of the inversions studied earlier. You might also choose the accompaniment style in which to perform the chords. Appendix H has numerous accompaniment patterns to try.

Hey Lidee

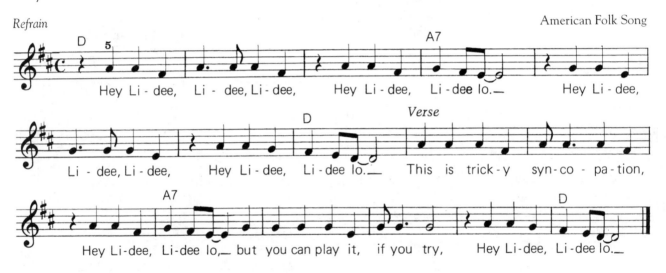

Saturday Night

Amazing Grace

John Newton (United States, 1725–1807)
Early American Melody

A - maz - ing_ grace how sweet the sound, that saved a_ wretch like me!_ I

once_ was_ lost but now_ am_ found, was blind but_ now I see._

Joy to the World

Isaac Watts
George F. Handel (Germany, 1685–1759)

Joy to the world, the Lord is come; Let earth re - ceive her King,_ Let

ev - 'ry_ heart_ pre - pare_ him_ room._ And heav'n and na - ture_ sing, And_

heav'n and na - ture_ sing, And_ heav'n_ and heav'n_ and na - ture sing.

St. James Infirmary

American Folk Song

I went down to St. James In - firm - 'ry_ I_ saw my ba - by_

there; All stretched out there on a ta - ble,_ so cold, so pale, and fair.

Worried Man Blues

American Folk Song

It takes a wor-ried man to sing a wor-ried song, It
takes a wor-ried man to sing a wor-ried song. It
takes a wor-ried man to sing a wor-ried song, I'm wor-ried
now, _____ But I won't be wor-ried long. _____

John B.

Caribbean Folk Song

Oh, we sailed on the sloop, John B., my grand-fath-er and me. 'Round Nas-sau
town we_ did roam._ Drink-in' all night,_ we got in a fight._ I
feel so break-up I want to go home._ So hoist up the John B. sails, and
see how the mains-s'l's set. Send for the cap-tain a - shore, lem-me go home,— lem-me go
home!_ Oh, lem-me go home!_ I feel so break-up, I want to go home._

Lucy in the Sky with Diamonds

John Lennon (England, 1940–1980)
Paul McCartney (England, b. 1942)

Traditional Mexican Song
Arranged by Joan Baez

De Colores

De___ co-lo-res, de co-lo-res se vis-ten los cam-pos en la pri-ma-ve-ra___
Can___ ta el ga-llo, can-ta el ga-llo con el qui-ri qui-ri qui-ri qui-ri qui-ri,___

___ De___ co-lo-res, de co-lo-res son las pa-ja-ri-tos, que vie-nen de a-
La___ ga-lli-na, la ga-lli-na con el ca-ra ca-ra ca-ra ca-ra

fue-ra,___ De___ co-lo-res, de co-lo-res es el ar-co
ca-ra,___ Los___ po-llue-los, los po-llue-los con el pi-o

ir-is que ve-mos lu-cir, y por e-so-los gran-des a-mo-res de mu-chos co-
pi-o pi-o pi-o pi

lo-res me gus-tan a mí. Y por e-so-los gran-des a-mo-res de mu-chos co-

1. lo-res me gus-tan a mí. 2. lo-res me gus-tan a mí.___

Aura Lee

American Folk Song

As the black-bird in the spring, 'Neath the wil - low tree, _____

Sat and piped, I heard him sing, Sing - ing Au - ra Lee.

Chorus

Au - ra Lee, Au - ra Lee, Maid of gol - den hair,

Sun - shine came a - long with thee, And swal - lows in the air.

This song was made into the popular song "Love Me Tender" (Elvis Presley).

John Lennon (England, 1940–1980)
Paul McCartney (England, b. 1942)

Michelle

Mi - chelle, ma belle, these are words that go to-geth-er well, my Mi - chelle,

Mi - chelle, ma belle, sont les mots qui vont très bien en-semble, très bien en-semble. I

love you, I love you, I love you. That's all I want to say. Un - til I find a
need you, I need you, I need you. I need to make you see. Oh, what you mean to
want you, I want you, I want you. I think you know by now. I'll get to you some-

way._____ I will say the on - ly words I know that you'll un - der - stand:
me._____ Un - til I do, I'm hop - ing you will know what I
how._____ Un - til I do, I'm tell - ing you so you'll un - der -

1. B

2. B *D. S. al coda*

mean. I

Coda

stand, my Mi - chelle.

John Lennon (England, 1940–1980)
Paul McCartney (England, b. 1942)

Yesterday

Yes - ter - day, all my troub - les seemed so far a - way,
Sud - den - ly, I'm not half the man I used to be,

Now it looks as if they're here to stay;_ Oh! I be - lieve_ in yes - ter - day._
There's a shad - ow hang - ing o - ver me;__ Oh! Yes - ter - day__ came sud - den - ly!__

Why she had to go I don't know, she would - n't say.

I said some - thing wrong, now I long for yes - ter - day._____

Yes - ter - day, love was such an eas - y game to play.

Now I need a place to hide a - way;_ Oh! I be - lieve_ in yes - ter - day._

ENSEMBLE MUSIC

Recreation I

Piano 2

Andante   Arnoldo Sartorio (Germany, 1853– ?)

Recreation I

Piano 1 *

Andante

Arnoldo Sartorio (Germany, 1853– ?)

*To perform Piano 1 with two students at a piano, one student plays the part as written while the second student plays the part two octaves lower.

280

Recreation II

Piano 2

Arnoldo Sartorio (Germany, 1853–?)

Andante cantabile

Recreation II

Piano 1

Andante cantabile

Arnoldo Sartorio (Germany, 1853–?)

J'ai du bon Tabac*

Piano 2

French Folk Song

Love Somebody*

Piano 2

American Folk Song

*These ensemble pieces marked for two pianos may also be performed on one piano by playing the Piano 1 part
an octave higher and the Piano 2 part an octave lower.

J'ai du bon Tabac

Piano 1

French Folk Song

Love Somebody

Piano 1

American Folk Song

Duet Exercise 32

Piano 2

Andante

Ferdinand Beyer (1803–1863)

Duet Exercise 32

Piano 1*

Andante   Ferdinand Beyer (1803–1863)

*To perform with two students at one piano, one student plays Piano 1 as written while another plays Piano 1 two octaves lower.

Waltz (from *Melodious Exercises*, Op. 62, No. 3)

Piano 2

Allegro

Hermann Berens (Germany, 1826–1880)

Waltz (from *Melodious Exercises*, Op. 62, No. 3)

Piano 1

Allegro

Hermann Berens (Germany, 1826–1880)

Duet Exercise 42

Piano 2

Andante

Ferdinand Beyer (1803–1863)

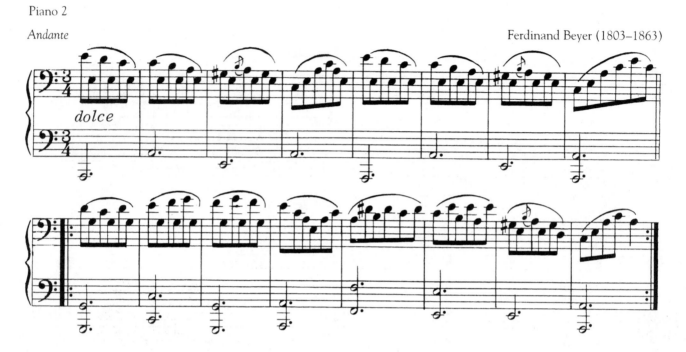

Duet Exercise 42

Piano 1*

Andante

Ferdinand Beyer (1803–1863)

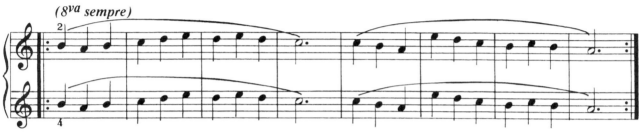

*To perform with two students at one piano, one student plays Piano 1 as written while another plays Piano 1
two octaves lower.

It's Natural to Have a Flat

Piano 2

Easy swing   Lee Evans (United States, b. 1933)

It's Natural to Have a Flat

Piano 1

Easy Swing

Lee Evans (United States, b. 1933)

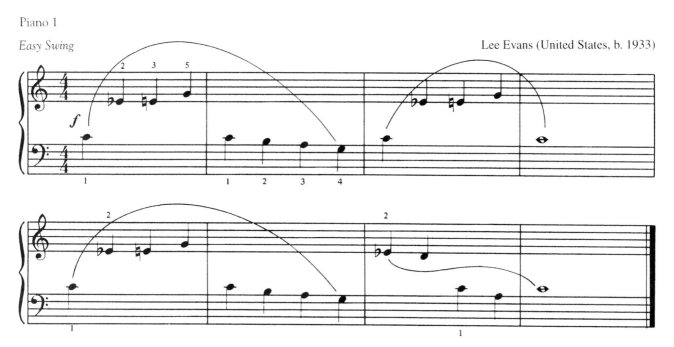

The **natural sign** (♮) cancels a flat or a sharp.

Etude, Op. 82, No. 11

Piano 2

Cornelius Gurlitt (Germany, 1820–1901)

Etude, Op. 82, No. 10

Piano 1

Cornelius Gurlitt (Germany, 1820–1901)

"Come, Follow" may be performed as a round with three groups of pianists.

Come, Follow

John Hilton (England, 1599–1657)
Arranged by Linda Mankin

Lively

Hello! Ma' Baby

Joseph E. Howard (United States, 1878–1961)
Ida Emerson (United States, late 19th–20th c.)

Piano 2

Hello! Ma' Baby

Joseph E. Howard (United States, 1878–1961)
Ida Emerson (United States, late 19th–20th c.)

Piano 1

Hel-lo! Ma' ba-by, Hel-lo! Ma' hon-ey. Hel-lo! My rag-time gal. Send me a kiss by

wire, Ba-by, my heart's on fire! If you re-fuse me, Hon-ey, you'll lose me,

Then you'll be left a-lone, oh! ba-by, Tel-e-phone and tell me you're my own.

Blue Jeans

Piano 2

Not too slowly (in 4)

Lee Evans (United States, b. 1933)

Blue Jeans

Piano 1

Not too slowly (in 4) (Both hands an octave higher when played as a duet.)   Lee Evans (United States, b. 1933)

Study (from Op. 823)

Piano 2

Carl Czerny (Austria, 1791–1857)

Linus and Lucy (Snoopy's Theme) (excerpt)

Piano 2

Vince Guaraldi
Arranged by Dee Spencer

Introduction

Study (from Op. 823)

Piano 1

Carl Czerny (Austria, 1791–1857)

Linus and Lucy (Snoopy's Theme) (excerpt)

Piano 1

Arranged by Dee Spencer

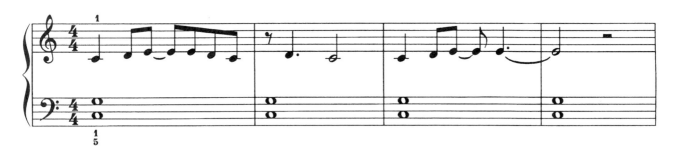

Shalom, Chaverim*

Piano 2

Israeli Round

Zum Gali Gali

Piano 2

Israeli Folk Melody

Zum ga-li, ga-li, ga-li, Zum ga-li, ga-li, Zum ga-li, ga-li, ga-li, Zum ga-li, ga-li,

He-cha lutz le 'man a-vo-dah, A-vo-dah le 'man-he-cha-lutz.

*"Shalom" may also be performed as a round. Piano 2 could play an introduction (last two measures of Piano 2 part), then play throughout and finish with a two-measure coda (same as introduction). Two groups of pianists could perform Piano 1 part. The second group could begin when the first has reached the last beat of measure 1. Repeat as many times as you wish. At one piano, play "Shalom" with Piano 1 part an octave higher and Piano 2 as notated.

Shalom, Chaverim

Piano 1

Israeli Round

Sha - lom, cha-ve-rim! Sha - lom, cha-ve-rim! Sha - lom, sha - lom! Le -

hit - ra - ot, le - hit - ra - ot, Sha - lom, sha - lom!

Zum Gali Gali

"Zum Gali Gali" may be performed by three groups of pianists* as follows:

Piano 1 Perform this ostinato for a two-measure introduction, throughout the piece, and as a two-measure coda.

Ostinato

Piano 2 After Piano 1's introduction, play "Zum Gali Gali."
Piano 3 Begin the melody when Piano 2 begins measure 5.

*At one piano, Piano 1 can be performed as written while Piano 2 is played an octave higher..

Scherzo from *Melodious Pieces* (Op. 149, No. 6)

Piano 2

Allegro   Anton Diabelli (Austria, 1781–1858)

Scherzo from *Melodious Pieces* (Op. 149, No. 6)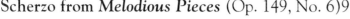9

Piano 1

Allegro

Anton Diabelli (Austria, 1781–1858)

Every Night When the Sun Goes In*

Piano 2

American Folk Song

*Play Piano 1 an octave higher and Piano 2 as notated for one piano and two pianists.

Every Night When the Sun Goes In

Piano 1

American Folk Song

Razzle Dazzle

Piano 2

Moderate swing   Lee Evans (United States, b. 1933)

Razzle Dazzle

Piano 1

Moderate swing

Lee Evans (United States, b. 1933)

Calico Rag

Piano 2

Dennis Alexander

Allegro moderato

Calico Rag

Piano 1 (may be performed one octave higher)

Allegro moderato

Dennis Alexander

APPENDIX A

Musical Terms and Signs

Dynamic Terms and Signs

pp Pianissimo: very soft

p Piano: soft

mp Mezzo piano: medium soft

mf Mezzo forte: medium loud

f Forte: loud

ff Fortissimo: very loud

< Crescendo (cresc.): gradually louder

> Decrescendo (decresc.): gradually softer

> Diminuendo (dim., dimin.): gradually softer

Common Tempo Terms

Largo: very slow

Lento: very slow

Adagio: slowly, leisurely

Larghetto: slow

Andante: moderately

Andantino: slightly faster than andante

Moderato: moderately

Allegretto: moderately fast

Allegro: fast, lively

Vivace: animated, lively

Presto: very rapidly

A tempo: return to original tempo

Accelerando (accel.): gradually increasing tempo

Rallentando (rall.): gradually becoming slower

Ritardando (rit.): gradually slower and slower

Ritenuto (riten.): immediately slowing in tempo

Additional Terms and Signs

Accent (>)

Affettuoso: with affection, warmth

Animato, animé: animated; with spirit

Assai: very

Calmado: calmly, tranquil

Cantabile: in singing style

Coda: a concluding section added to the end of a composition

Commodo: conveniently, quietly, easily

Con: with

Con anima: with animation

Con moto: with motion

Con spirito: with spirit

D.C. (Da capo): repeat from the beginning

D.C. al coda (Da capo al coda): return to the beginning and play to the measure marked with coda sign (⊕), concluding with coda

D.C. al fine (Da capo al fine): return to the beginning and conclude with the measure marked *fine*

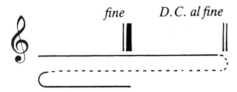

D.S. (Dal segno): repeat from the sign 𝄋

D.S. al coda (Dal segno al coda): return to the sign 𝄋 and conclude with the coda

D.S. al fine (Dal segno al fine): return to the sign 𝄋 and conclude with the measure marked *fine*

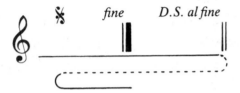

Dolce: sweetly, softly

Espressivo: with expression

Fermata (⌢): hold or pause

Fine: the end

Giocoso: playfully, humorously

Grazioso: gracefully

Legato: smoothly, connected

Leggiero: light, delicate

Loco: place; play as written

Lunga: prolonged pause

Ma non troppo: but not too much

Maestoso: majestically

Marcia: in the style of a march

Meno: less

Molto: much

Mosso: agitated

Moto: motion; speed; movement

Nicht schnell: not fast

Ottava alta (8va ⁻⁻⁻⁊): play an octave higher than written

Ottava bassa (8va _ _ ⌋): play an octave lower than written

Pastorale: simple, tender, flowing

Per: for, by, from, in

Pesante: heavily

Piú: more

Poco: little

Preciso: precise

Rinforzando (rf., rfz.): pronounced accent or stress

Risoluto: resolute, bold

Ritmo: rhythm

Rubato: flexibility of tempo with slight ritards for musical expression

Scherzando: playful

Sempre: always, continually

Sforzando (sf., sfz.): a strong accent

Simile: in a similar manner

Sostenuto: sustained

Spirito: spirit, life

Staccato (♪): short, detached

Subito: suddenly, at once

Tenuto (♩): sustain for full value

Tranquillo: calm, quiet

Très expressif: very expressive

Tutti: all (singular: tutto)

Un: one

Valse: waltz

Vivo: lively, spiritedly, briskly

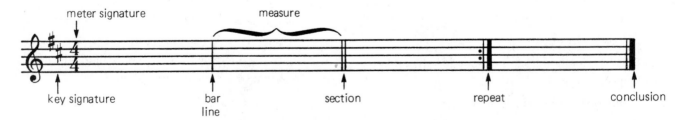

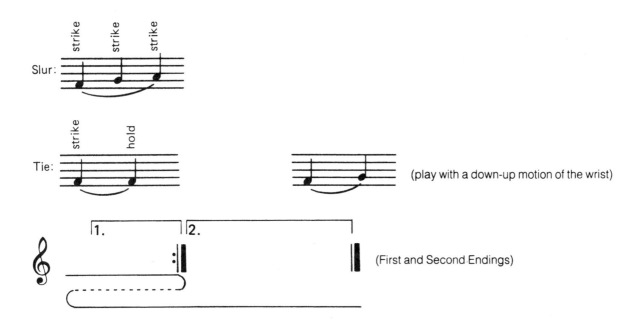

Slur:

strike   strike   strike

Tie:

strike   hold

(play with a down-up motion of the wrist)

1.   2.

(First and Second Endings)

♩ = 80   Tempos are often indicated in *metronome markings*. This example indicates that a metronome (a mechanical device ticking at a desired speed) should be set at 80. The ♩ will be equal to 80 beats or ticks per minute on a metronome.

Treble and Bass Clef Notation

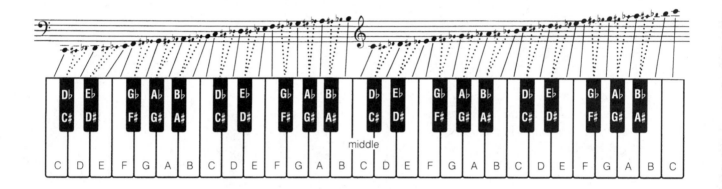

Circle of Fifths (Major and Minor Keys)

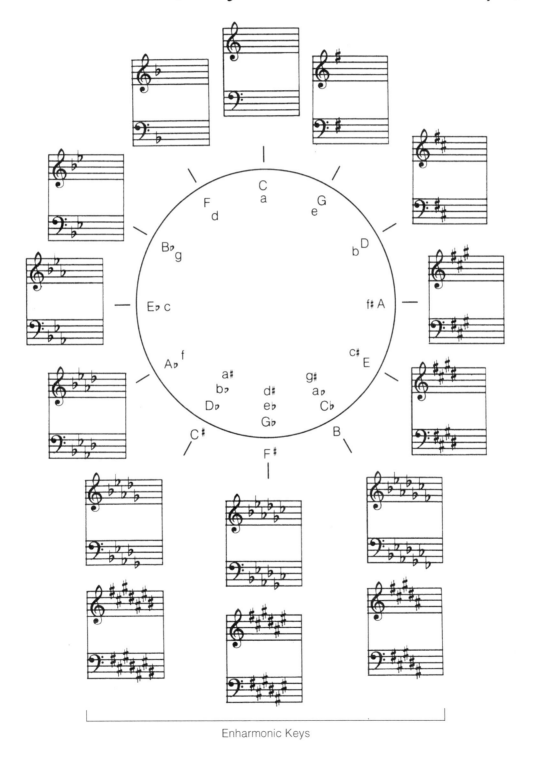

Enharmonic Keys

Major Scales

Major Scale Degrees

Number	Name
1	*Tonic*
2	*Supertonic* (one whole step above the tonic)
3	*Mediant* (between 1 and 5 and a third above the tonic)
4	*Subdominant* (a fifth below the tonic)
5	*Dominant* (a fifth above the tonic)
6	*Submediant* (a third below the tonic)
7	*Leading tone* (a half step below the tonic)

Major Scales (with Piano Fingerings)

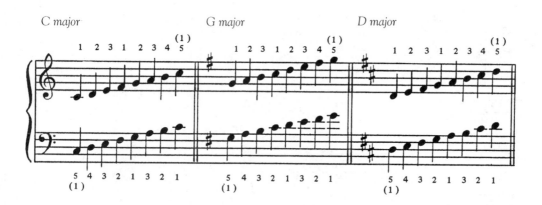

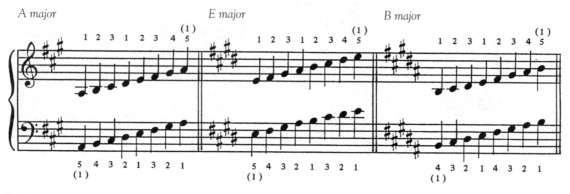

F♯ major C♯ major

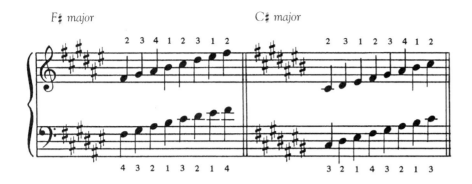

F major B♭ major E♭ major

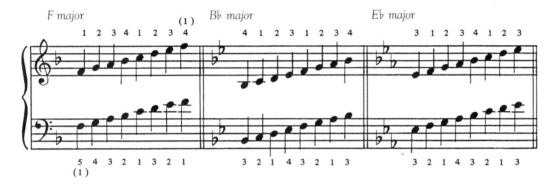

A♭ major D♭ major

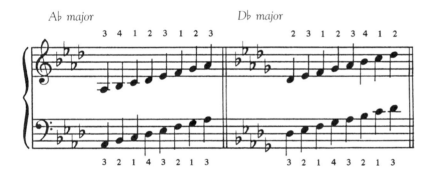

G♭ major C♭ major

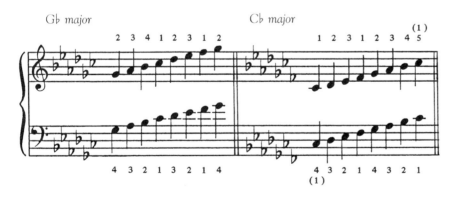

Major Scales (Fingerings for two-octave scales)

Scale	Fingering		
C major	RH	1 2 3 1 2 3 4	1 2 3 1 2 3 4 5
	LH	5 4 3 2 1 3 2	1 4 3 2 1 3 2 1
G major	RH	1 2 3 1 2 3 4̇	1 2 3 1 2 3 4̇ 5
	LH	5 4 3 2 1 3 2̇	1 4 3 2 1 3 2̇ 1
D major	RH	1 2 3̇ 1 2 3 4̇	1 2 3̇ 1 2 3 4̇ 5
	LH	5 4 3̇ 2 1 3 2̇	1 4 3̇ 2 1 3 2̇ 1
A major	RH	1 2 3̇ 1 2 3̇ 4	1 2 3̇ 1 2 3̇ 4 5
	LH	5 4 3̇ 2 1 3 2̇	1 4 3̇ 2 1 3 2̇ 1
E major	RH	1 2̇ 3̇ 1 2 3̇ 4	1 2̇ 3̇ 1 2 3̇ 4 5
	LH	5 4̇ 3̇ 2 1 3̇ 2	1 4̇ 3̇ 2 1 3̇ 2 1
B major	RH	1 2̇ 3̇ 1 2̇ 3̇ 4	1 2̇ 3̇ 1 2̇ 3̇ 4 5
	LH	4 3̇ 2̇ 1 4 3̇ 2	1 3̇ 2̇ 1 4 3̇ 2 1
F♯ major	RH	2̇ 3̇ 4̇ 1 2̇ 3̇ 1	2̇ 3̇ 4̇ 1 2̇ 3̇ 1 2̇
	LH	4̇ 3̇ 2̇ 1 3̇ 2̇ 1	4̇ 3̇ 2̇ 1 3̇ 2̇ 1 4̇
C♯ major	RH	2̇ 3̇ 1 2̇ 3̇ 4̇ 1	2̇ 3̇ 1 2̇ 3̇ 4̇ 1 2̇
	LH	3̇ 2̇ 1 4̇ 3̇ 2̇ 1	3̇ 2̇ 1 4̇ 3̇ 2̇ 1 3̇
F major	RH	1 2 3 4̇ 1 2 3	1 2 3 4̇ 1 2 3 4
	LH	5 4 3 2̇ 1 3 2	1 4 3 2̇ 1 3 2 1
B♭ major	RH	4̇ 1 2 3̇ 1 2 3	4̇ 1 2 3̇ 1 2 3 4̇
	LH	3̇ 2 1 4̇ 3 2 1	3̇ 2 1 4̇ 3 2 1 3̇
E♭ major	RH	3̇ 1 2 3̇ 4̇ 1 2	3̇ 1 2 3̇ 4̇ 1 2 3̇
	LH	3̇ 2 1 4̇ 3̇ 2 1	3̇ 2 1 4̇ 3̇ 2 1 3̇
A♭ major	RH	3̇ 4̇ 1 2̇ 3̇ 1 2	3̇ 4̇ 1 2̇ 3̇ 1 2 3̇
	LH	3̇ 2̇ 1 4̇ 3̇ 2 1	3̇ 2̇ 1 4̇ 3̇ 2 1 3̇
D♭ major	RH	2̇ 3̇ 1 2̇ 3̇ 4̇ 1	2̇ 3̇ 1 2̇ 3̇ 4̇ 1 2̇
	LH	3̇ 2̇ 1 4̇ 3̇ 2̇ 1	3̇ 2̇ 1 4̇ 3̇ 2̇ 1 3̇
G♭ major	RH	2̇ 3̇ 4̇ 1 2̇ 3̇ 1	2̇ 3̇ 4̇ 1 2̇ 3̇ 1 2̇
	LH	4̇ 3̇ 2̇ 1 3̇ 2̇ 1	4̇ 3̇ 2̇ 1 3̇ 2̇ 1 4̇
C♭ major	RH	1 2̇ 3̇ 1 2̇ 3̇ 4̇	1 2̇ 3̇ 1 2̇ 3̇ 4̇ 5
	LH	4̇ 3̇ 2̇ 1 4̇ 3̇ 2̇	1 3̇ 2̇ 1 4̇ 3̇ 2̇ 1

• = black key

Minor Scales

Minor Scale Degrees

Number	Name
1	*Tonic*
2	*Supertonic* (one whole step above the tonic)
3	*Mediant* (a third above the tonic)
4	*Subdominant* (a fifth below the tonic)
5	*Dominant* (a fifth above the tonic)
6	*Submediant* (a third below the tonic)
7	*Leading tone* (a half step below the tonic)
	or
	Subtonic (a whole step below the tonic)

Selected Minor Scales (with Piano Fingerings)

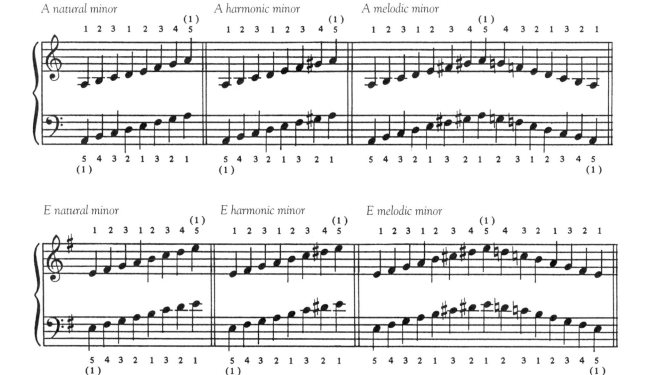

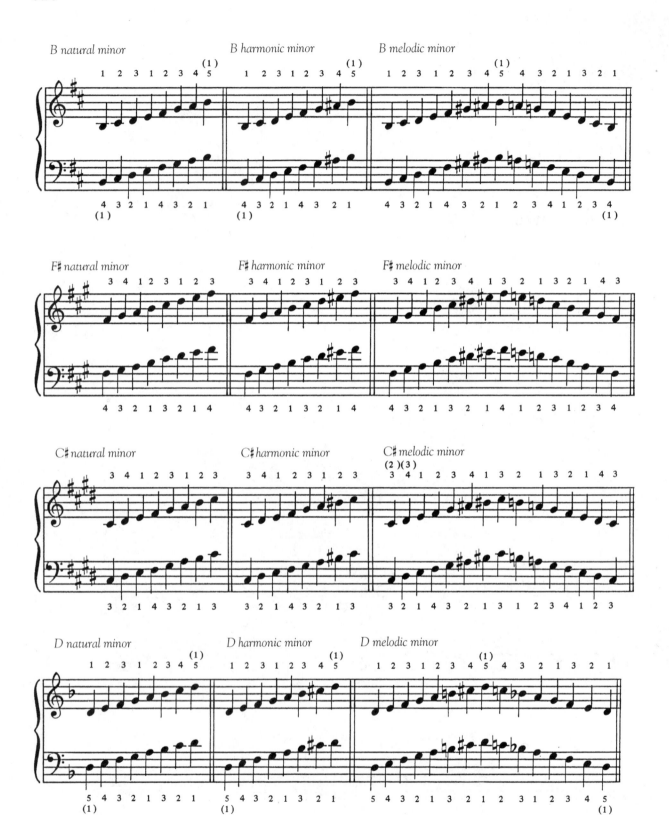

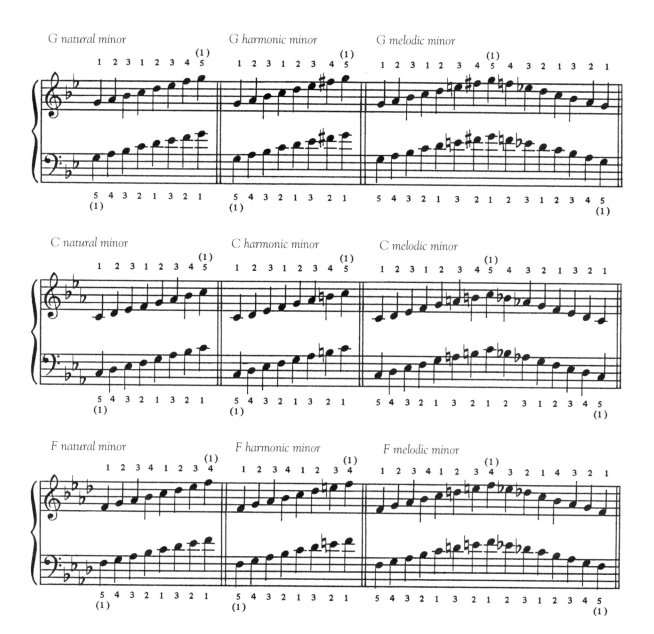

Selected Harmonic Minor Scales
(Fingerings for two-octave scales)

Scale	Fingering		
A harmonic	RH 1 2 3 1 2 3 4̇	1 2 3 1 2 3 4̇ 5
	LH 5 4 3 2 1 3 2̇	1 4 3 2 1 3 2̇ 1
E harmonic	RH 1 2̇ 3 1 2 3 4̇	1 2̇ 3 1 2 3 4̇ 5
	LH 5 4̇ 3 2 1 3 2̇	1 4̇ 3 2 1 3 2̇ 1
B harmonic	RH 1 2̇ 3 1 2̇ 3 4̇	1 2̇ 3 1 2 3 4̇ 5
	LH 4 3̇ 2 1 4̇ 3 2̇	1 3̇ 2 1 4 3 2̇ 1
F♯ harmonic	RH 3̇ 4̇ 1 2 3̇ 1 2	3̇ 4̇ 1 2 3̇ 1 2 3̇
	LH 4̇ 3̇ 2 1 3̇ 2 1	4̇ 3̇ 2 1 3̇ 2 1 4̇
C♯ harmonic	RH 3̇ 4̇ 1 2̇ 3̇ 1 2	3̇ 4̇ 1 2̇ 3̇ 1 2 3̇
	LH 3̇ 2̇ 1 4̇ 3̇ 2 1	3̇ 2̇ 1 4̇ 3̇ 2 1 3̇
D harmonic	RH 1 2 3 1 2 3̇ 4̇	1 2 3 1 2 3̇ 4̇ 5
	LH 5 4 3 2 1 3̇ 2̇	1 4 3 2 1 3̇ 2̇ 1
G harmonic	RH 1 2 3̇ 1 2 3 4̇	1 2 3̇ 1 2 3 4̇ 5
	LH 5 4 3̇ 2 1 3 2̇	1 4 3̇ 2 1 3 2̇ 1
C harmonic	RH 1 2 3̇ 1 2 3̇ 4	1 2 3̇ 1 2 3̇ 4 5
	LH 5 4 3̇ 2 1 3̇ 2	1 4 3̇ 2 1 3̇ 2 1
F harmonic	RH 1 2 3̇ 4̇ 1 2̇ 3	1 2 3̇ 4̇ 1 2̇ 3 4
	LH 5 4 3̇ 2̇ 1 3̇ 2	1 4 3̇ 2̇ 1 3̇ 2 1

• = black key

APPENDIX F

Intervals and Chords

Intervals

An *interval* is the pitch distance between two tones. Intervals are identified by the number of steps they encompass and by quality. The five qualities are as follows: perfect (P), major (M), minor (m), diminished (d or °), and augmented (A or +).

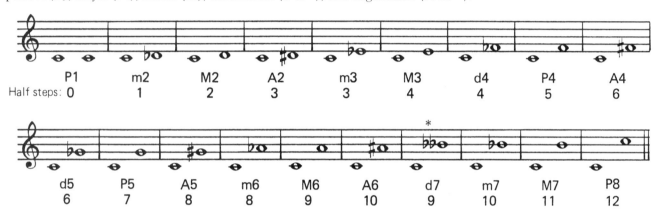

	P1	m2	M2	A2	m3	M3	d4	P4	A4
Half steps:	0	1	2	3	3	4	4	5	6

	d5	P5	A5	m6	M6	A6	d7	m7	M7	P8
	6	7	8	8	9	10	9	10	11	12

Triads

The four kinds of triads (three-note chords) are *major, minor, augmented,* and *diminished.*

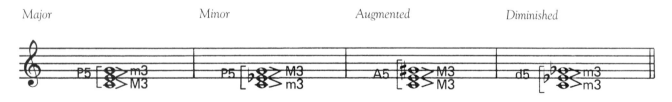

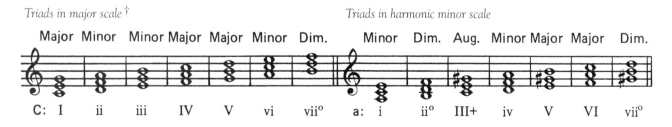

Triads in major scale †

Major	Minor	Minor	Major	Major	Minor	Dim.
C: I	ii	iii	IV	V	vi	vii°

Triads in harmonic minor scale

Minor	Dim.	Aug.	Minor	Major	Major	Dim.
a: i	ii°	III+	iv	V	VI	vii°

*♭♭ (**double flat**). A double flat lowers a pitch one whole step.

†Chords built on steps 1, 4, and 5 of a major or a minor scale are primary chords. Chords built on steps 2, 3, 6, and 7 are **secondary chords.**

Seventh Chords

The seventh chord consists of four notes: a triad with an added third. There are five types of seventh chords: *major-minor, major-major, minor-minor, diminished-minor,* and *diminished-diminished.* Each seventh chord also has a common name, shown in the following chart. Use the terms recommended by your instructor. See also Appendix I.

Seventh Chord Type	Symbols	Common Name
Major-minor seventh	7 or Mm7	Dominant seventh
Major-major seventh	maj7 or MM7	Major seventh
Minor-minor seventh	m7 or mm7	Minor seventh
Diminished-minor seventh	half-dim7	Half-diminished seventh
Diminished-diminished seventh	dim7 or dd7	Diminished seventh

Major-minor (dominant) seventh chord

Major-major seventh chord

Minor-minor seventh chord

Half-diminished seventh chord

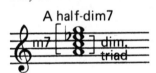

Diminished seventh chord

APPENDIX G

Selected Primary Chords

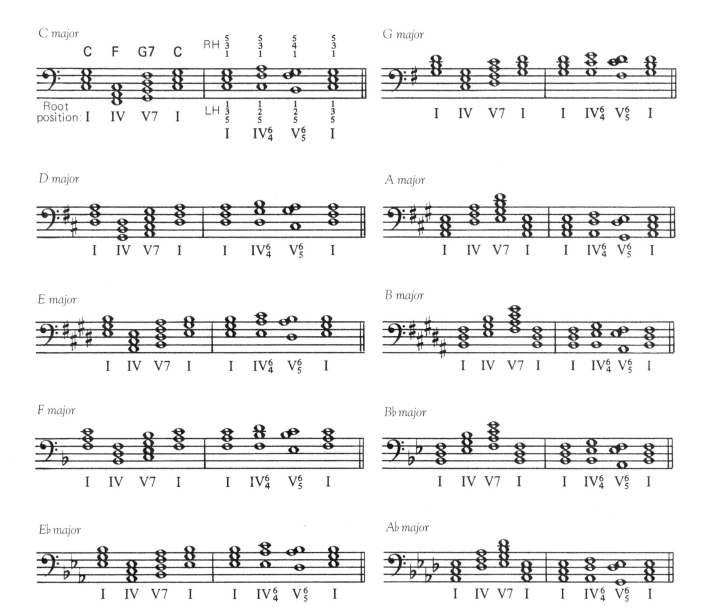

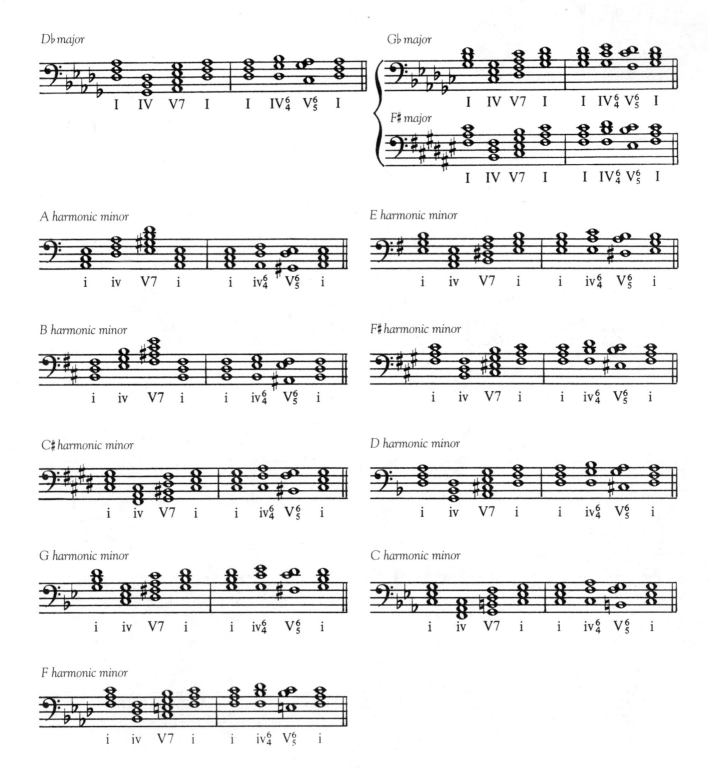

APPENDIX H

Accompaniment Patterns

1. Chord roots

2. Drone, or open fifths

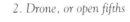

3. Block chord

4a. Broken chord in 2

4b. Broken chord in 3

4c. Broken chord in 4

5. Broken chord, Alberti bass

6a. Arpeggio in 2

6b. Arpeggio in 3

6c. Arpeggio in 4

6d. Arpeggio in 6

14. Funk-rock bass

15. Blues bass

16. Western bass

17. Walking bass

18. Rock rhythm

19. Rock ostinato

20. Habañera

Chords and Chord Symbols (Lead Sheet Notation)

Key for Chord Symbols

1. A capital letter indicates a major triad.

2. A capital letter followed by a lowercase *m* indicates a minor triad.

3. A capital letter followed by *dim* or a small circle (°) indicates a diminished triad.

4. A capital letter followed by *aug* or a plus sign (+) indicates an augmented triad.

5. When any of the preceding letters and symbols are followed by the numeral 7, a seventh chord is indicated. (See also Appendix F.)

6. When any of the preceding letters and symbols are followed by a 6, a major sixth is added above the root.

✗ (double sharp). A double sharp raises a pitch one whole step.

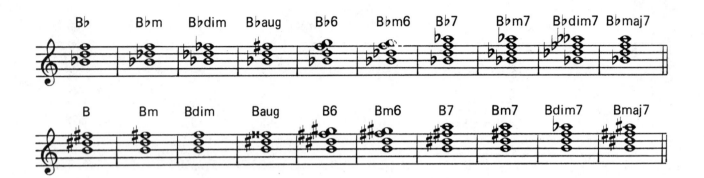

Chords over Bass Notes

In jazz and popular music, chords are often superimposed over a bass note. In such cases, two capital letters, separated by a slash (/), are used—for example, C/G or Cm7/F. The first symbol indicates the chord to be played and the second symbol specifies the bass notes.

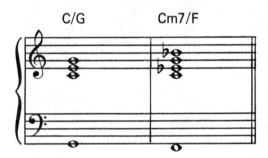

APPENDIX J

Electronic Keyboards

Electronic keyboards may be grouped into three categories: *basic keyboards, digital pianos,* and *synthesizers.*

Basic Keyboards

Basic keyboards are the most commonly purchased (and the least costly) nonprofessional electronic keyboards. Their most attractive features, outside of price, are battery operation, portability, and self-contained speaker systems. In addition, all basic keyboards include preprogrammed rhythmic accompaniments and automatic chordal accompaniments.

Preprogrammed Rhythmic Accompaniments

Basic keyboards typically offer approximately ten to twenty preprogrammed rhythm patterns (percussion only—no pitched sounds). For example, one preprogrammed rhythmic accompaniment might be an eight-beat pattern of one to two measures of eighth notes in $\frac{4}{4}$. This pattern could be used as a rhythmic accompaniment for a rock, soul, or pop song. Most preprogrammed accompaniments feature a drum set and a variety of percussion instruments. Although the choices are labeled, some experimentation is often necessary to find the correct rhythmic accompaniment for a particular song.

Virtually all keyboards allow the player to vary the tempo of the selected rhythm. A player should experiment with tempo and rhythmic combinations to make the appropriate accompaniment choice.

Automatic and Fingered Chordal Accompaniments

Most basic keyboards offer a split keyboard (one that is divided into two or more sections), with the lower one and one-half octaves serving as the on-demand automatic accompaniment section. When the automatic accompaniment function is activated, a chordal accompaniment and a bass line are added to the selected rhythm in the proper style and tempo.

In the "fingered" or manual mode, the player must play (and finger) all the notes in the chord. Again, the style and tempo of the actual chordal accompaniment depends on the selected rhythm.

Manual or Fingered Mode

Fingered—C chord   *Actual sound (8-beat rhythm pattern)*

The "one-touch" mode allows the player to *depress only the chord root* to sound a major triad accompaniment (once the selected rhythm is activated).

"One-Touch" Mode

Fingered—C chord   *Sound (no rhythm)*

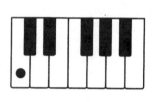

Other chords may be sounded by depressing additional keys. For example, the systems made by Casio and Yamaha, two major manufacturers of electronic keyboards, differ in the selection of additional keys to sound the various chords. In the Casio system, the root of the chord is always the lowest note fingered and a major triad is automatically sounded. By depressing any combination of one, two, or three *higher* pitches (*as long as they are within the accompaniment section of the split keyboard*), the player may sound the minor triad, the major-minor seventh chord, and minor seventh chord variations.

Casio System

Fingered—Cm chord   *Sound*   *Fingered—C7 chord*   *Sound*

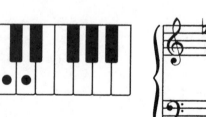
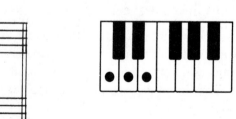

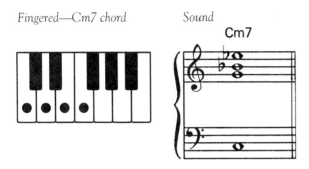

Fingered—Cm7 chord   *Sound*

In the Yamaha system, *any* white key added that is *lower* than the root will change the major triad to a major-minor seventh chord (dominant seventh chord); *any* black key *lower* than the root will change it to a minor triad.

Yamaha System

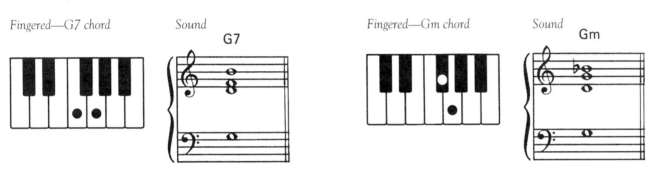

Fingered—G7 chord   *Sound*   *Fingered—Gm chord*   *Sound*

Performance Suggestions for Fingered and Touch Modes

1. In both fingered and "one-touch" modes, there is no need to hold down a key (or keys) to repeat a chordal accompaniment *as long as the selected rhythm is activated*.

2. Some songs may be accompanied with a rhythmic pattern, and others may sound better without a preprogrammed rhythmic accompaniment. Therefore, two styles of LH playing are necessary.

   a. When using rhythmic accompaniments in both the fingered and the "one-touch" modes, it is not necessary or advisable to hold down a key(s) to repeat a chordal accompaniment.

   b. When the rhythmic function is not used, the keys must be depressed continuously by the player. (Some timbre choices on the keyboard will naturally include more sustain than others—for example, violin and organ.) Once again, experimentation is important.

3. In the fingered mode, the player may use chord inversions without altering the root in the bass. This is an effective feature that makes LH chording much easier for the beginning and the intermediate player.

It takes considerable practice and patience to learn the individual idiosyncrasies of an electronic keyboard. However, portable basic keyboards offer many features that can develop one's musical understanding, as well as features that make playing more fun and interesting.

Digital Pianos

Unlike basic keyboards and synthesizers, digital pianos are distinguishable because they have the look and, more important, the feel (weighted action) of a conventional acoustic piano. One of the important differences is a digital piano's MIDI (Musical Instrument Digital Interface) capabilities. This capability allows it to be used as a controller keyboard for other MIDI instruments, allows a performer to "record" a melody and then "play" it back at the touch of a button (called *sequencing*), and offers choices of preprogrammed timbres. The timbre choices might include the distinctive sounds of specific brands of pianos, organ sounds, or string sounds. Some even offer the capability to make the instrument sound as though it is being played in a room, on a stage, or in a large concert hall. Performance techniques for digital pianos, when employing an acoustic piano sound, are the same as for any acoustic piano.

Synthesizers

Synthesizers, the most electronically sophisticated of the three groups of instruments, offer far more options for programmability than either basic keyboards or digital pianos. They also come in many styles, types, and sizes.

Generally, synthesizers do not include preprogrammed rhythmic accompaniments, self-contained speaker systems, or automatic chording. Some do specialize in sampling (a digital "recording" of any acoustic sound), and others include onboard sequencers, as opposed to a separate electronic sequencing device like a computer. Performance techniques for synthesizers are quite different from those used for acoustic and digital pianos, mostly because of the lighter, organlike action. Ultimately, instrument or timbre selection will dictate performance techniques.

Recent synthesizer and basic keyboard models include internal sequencers that can be programmed. The sequencing process involves the layering of two or more sound patterns or tracks—each part entered one at a time. Each track contains a specific instrument performance that is stored. When many tracks are layered and stored, a sequence program is created. Some *sequencers* allow for additional fine tuning of pitches and tempi.

A typical sequence program for a jazz or a popular song contains the following basic tracks:

1. Rhythmic drum pattern
2. Bass pattern
3. Chordal accompaniment pattern
4. Melody

The following example illustrates a three-track sequence program for Duke Ellington's "It Don't Mean a Thing if It Ain't Got That Swing" (p. 264).

Track 1: Drum pattern—"swing" feel (choose a medium tempo for 8 measures).

Track 2: Bass pattern—LH bass clef part (choose an appropriate patch sound).

Track 3: Melody—RH treble clef part (choose an appropriate patch sound).

Criteria for Purchasing Electronic Keyboards

When purchasing an electronic keyboard to use primarily for developing piano skills, one should keep in mind the following:

Touch-sensitive keyboard actions are better for learning how to control dynamic levels and are most like the touch of an acoustic piano.

Keyboards that feature keys equivalent in size to standard acoustic piano keys are more comfortable for developing a good hand position.

Keyboards with just a few features in tone qualities and automatic rhythms (as opposed to an elaborate set of choices) may be sufficient and preferable for beginning keyboard study.

Selected Bibliography

Anderton, Craig. *Midi for Musicians.* New York: AMSCO Publications, 1986.

Crombie, David. *The New Complete Synthesizer.* London: Omnibus Press, 1986.

Hurtig, Brent, ed. *Synthesizers and Computers.* Rev. ed. Cupertino, Calif.: GPI Publications, 1987.

Mash, David. *Computers and the Music Educator.* Menlo Park, Calif.: Digidesign Inc., 1991.

Yelton, Geary. *The Rock Synthesizer Manual.* Woodstock, Ga.: Rock Tech Publications, 1986.

Timeline of Western Art Music and History

Musical Style Periods	Medieval ca. 500–ca. 1420	Renaissance ca. 1420–ca. 1600	Baroque ca. 1600–ca. 1750
Music Elements	*Melody:* moves mostly in steps; limited vocal range; uses church modes	*Melody:* moves mostly in steps; expanded vocal range	*Melody:* moves in steps and skips; sequential; use of ornamentation
	Harmony: monophonic; polyphonic for 2 to 4 voices; use of imitation in 14th c.	*Harmony:* 4 parts; use of imitation; dissonance (cadence points); text painting	*Harmony:* major-minor scales; polyphonic; homophonic; chord progressions I–IV–V
	Rhythm: moves in free chant rhythm; beat groupings of 3s in 13th c.; beat groupings of 2s in 14th c.	*Rhythm:* beat groupings of 2s; syncopation; more complex rhythms	*Rhythm:* free (recitative); steady, clear meters
	Form: free vocal chant forms; songs with verses, hymns; free and fixed poetic forms for secular music	*Form:* fixed poetic forms are replaced by imitation; songs with verses; hymns	*Form:* A B and A B A; fugue; development of multimovement compositions
	Timbre: small choirs (monophonic chants); soloists (polyphonic music); instrumental music (generally improvised)	*Timbre:* polyphonic; 5 or more voices in 16th c.; homophony; music for specific instruments; secular: soloists, small ensembles; sacred: small choirs, polyphony	*Timbre:* small choral groups; small orchestras—strings, winds, continuo; soloists
Types of Compositions	mass; plainchant setting of parts of the mass; motet (mostly secular); secular songs; instrumental dances	polyphonic settings of parts of mass; motet; secular songs; instrumental dances; instrumental pieces	mass and motet with instrumental accompaniment; opera; cantata; oratario; sonata; concerto; fugue; suite
Music and Historical Events and Figures	Benedictine Order founded (ca. 530)	Invention of printing press (ca. 1440)	First Black slaves to U.S.A. (1619)
	First Crusade (1096–1099)	Beginning of music printing (ca. 1500)	Harvard University (1636)
	Alhambra Palace (1238–1358)	Leonardo da Vinci (1452–1519)	First public opera house (Venice, 1637)
	Marco Polo travels to China (1271)	Michelangelo (1475–1564)	Isaac Newton (1642–1727)
	Dante (1265–1321)	Columbus discovers America (1492)	Bashō (poet, 1644–1694)
	Chaucer (ca. 1340–1400)	The Reformation (1517)	Reign of Louis XIV (1643–1715)
		Shakespeare (1564–1616)	Reign of Peter the Great (1682–1725)
			Early pianoforte (1709)

Classic ca. 1750–ca. 1820	Romantic ca. 1820–ca. 1900	Contemporary ca. 1900–
Melody: motivic; short phrases, 8-bar phrases	*Melody:* lyrical; phrases less regular; longer phrases	*Melody:* tone rows
Harmony: major-minor scales; use of modulation; change of key within a movement; homophony	*Harmony:* major-minor scales; expanded use of modulation and chromaticism; harmony; counterpoint	*Harmony:* major-minor sacles; atonal; new methods of tonal harmony; homophony; counterpoint; polytonality
Rhythm: free (recitative), clear meters; rhythmic variety	*Rhythm:* variety of meters; varied rhythmic patterns; meter change within movements	*Rhythm:* variety of meters; varied rhythmic patterns; shifting meter, asymmetric meter
Form: sonata; rondo; theme and variations; A B and A B A; multimovement compositions	*Form:* multimovement works; classical forms are expanded	*Form:* forms of all previous periods are used, with extensive changes; freer forms developed
Timbre: instruments more prominent than voice; larger orchestras—without use of continuo	*Timbre:* growth of orchestra; large chorus; large bands; small ensembles	*Timbre:* same as previous period; large bands; emphasis on percussive sound
mass; oratorio; opera; solo concerto; unaccompanied sonata; instrumental works: symphony, concerto, sonata, string quartet	classical forms are expanded; symphonic poem; solo song cycle; piano character piece	forms from all previous periods are used and expanded; impressionism; expressionism; electronic music; minimalism
Benjamin Franklin (1706–1790) George Washington (1732–1799) Goethe (1749–1832) Development of string quartet (ca. 1750) Industrial Revolution (ca. 1770) American Declaration of Independence (1776) French Revolution (1789)	Darwin (1809–1882) Dickens (1812–1870) Marx (1818–1883) Victoria (1819–1901) Freud (1856–1939) Invention of phonograph (1877) Einstein (1879–1955)	Airplane invented (1903) World War I (1914–1918) Russian Revolution (1917) First recordings of jazz (1917) Television (1929) Martin Luther King, Jr. (1929–1968) World War II (1939–1945) Invention of long-playing records (1948) Development of indeterminate music (1950s) Beatles come to U.S.A. (1963) Moon walk (1969) Berlin Wall falls (1989)

Timeline of Selected Keyboard Composers and Keyboard Instruments

Keyboard Composers

Musical Style Periods	Medieval ca. 500–ca. 1420	Renaissance ca. 1420–ca. 1600	Baroque ca. 1600–ca. 1750
	Landini (1325–1397)	Tallis (ca. 1505–1585)	Schütz (1585–1672)
	Paumann (ca. 1410–1473)	Cabezón (1510–1566)	Scheidt (1587–1654)
		A. Gabrieli (ca 1533–1585)	Hilton (1599–1657)
		C. Merulo (1533–1604)	Froberger (1616–1667)
		Morley (1557–1602)	Lully (1632–1687)
		Bull (1562–1628)	Buxtehude (1637–1707)
		Sweelinck (1562–1621)	Pachelbel (1653–1706)
		O. Gibbons (1583–1625)	de La Guerre (1659–1729)
			Purcell (ca. 1659–1695)
			Couperin (1668–1733)
			Telemann (1681–1767)
			Rameau (1683–1764)
			Handel (1685–1759)
			J. S. Bach (1685–1750)
			D. Scarlatti (1685–1757)
			---------(Pre-Classic)---------
			W. F. Bach (1710–1784)
			C.P.E. Bach (1714–1788)
			L. Mozart (1719–1787)
			J.C.F. Bach (1732–1795)
			Kirnberger (1721–1783)

Classic ca. 1750–ca. 1820	Romantic ca. 1820–ca. 1900	Contemporary ca. 1900–
Haydn (1732–1809)	Schubert (1797–1828)	Debussy (1862–1918)
Martines (1744–1812)	L. Farrenc (1804–1875)	Satie (1866–1925)
Türk (1750–1813)	Fanny Mendelssohn Hensel (1805–1847)	Beach (1867–1944)
Clementi (1752–1832)	Felix Mendelssohn (1809–1847)	Joplin (1868–1917)
W. A. Mozart (1756–1791)	Chopin (1810–1849)	Scriabin (1872–1915)
Müller (1767–1817)	R. Schumann (1810–1856)	Rachmaninoff (1873–1943)
----------------------------------	Liszt (1811–1886)	Schoenberg (1874–1951)
	Kunz (1812–1875)	Ravel (1875–1937)
Beethoven (1770–1827)	C. Schumann (1819–1896)	de Falla (1876–1946)
Diabelli (1781–1858)	Köhler (1820–1886)	Bloch (1880–1959)
Kuhlau (1786–1832)	Hanon (1820–1900)	Bartók (1881–1945)
M. Szymanowska (1789–1831)	Gurlitt (1820–1901)	Stravinsky (1882–1971)
Czerny (1791–1857)	Franck (1822–1890)	Webern (1883–1945)
	Berens (1826–1880)	"Jellyroll" Morton (1885–1941)
	Gottschalk (1829–1869)	Niebergall (1886–1968)
	Brahms (1833–1897)	Prokofiev (1891–1953)
	Saint-Saëns (1835–1921)	Milhaud (1892–1974)
	Mussorgsky (1839–1881)	Cowell (1897–1965)
	Tchaikovsky (1840–1893)	Gershwin (1898–1937)
	Dvořák (1841–1904)	Copland (1900–1990)
	Grieg (1843–1907)	Kabalevsky (1904–1987)
	Sartorio (1853– ?)	"Fats" Waller (1904–1943)
	----------------------------------	Shostakovich (1906–1975)
		Finney (b. 1906)
	Janáček (1854–1928)	Cage (1912–1992)
	MacDowell (1860–1908)	Persichetti (1915–1987)
	Rebikov (1866–1920)	Monk (1918–1982)
	K. Szymanowski (1882–1937)	Diemer (b. 1927)
		Musgrave (b. 1928)
		Bielawa (b. 1930)
		Van de Vate (b. 1930)
		Biggs (b. 1932)
		Evans (b. 1937)
		Olson (1938–1987)
		T. Johnson (b. 1939)
		Jarrett (b. 1945)

The Development of Keyboard Instruments

Medieval ca. 500–ca. 1420	Renaissance ca. 1420–ca. 1600	Baroque ca. 1600–ca. 1750
Organ (portative/positive)		Simplified church organ (pipe)
	Fretted clavichord	Unfretted clavichord
	Harpsichord	
	Virginal	

Classic ca 1750–ca. 1820   Romantic ca. 1820–ca. 1900   Contemporary ca. 1900–

Electronic (rotary-powered organ)

Pianoforte   Upright piano   Electronic piano

Celesta

Synthesizer   Electronic keyboards

Digital piano

APPENDIX M

Biographical Sketches of *PianoLab* Composers

Brief information on selected composers follows. For more complete biographical information, consult reference sources such as *Baker's Biographical Dictionary of Musicians* and *The New Grove Dictionary of Music and Musicians*.

Bach, Carl Philipp Emanuel (Germany 1714–1788): Brilliant keyboard performer at the court of Frederick the Great; son of J. S. Bach; composed keyboard works, orchestral works, and concertos; author of the important treatise *Essay on the True Art of Playing Keyboard Instruments* (1753).

Bach, Johann Christoph Friedrich (Germany, 1732–1795): Composer and court chamber musician at Bückeburg, Germany; son of J. S. Bach; composed chamber and keyboard music, keyboard concertos, cantatas, and oratorios.

Bach, Johann Sebastian (Germany, 1685–1750): Outstanding composer of the late Baroque period; wrote cantatas, passions, and other choral works; organ, harpsichord, and clavichord works; chamber and orchestral music; harmonized hundreds of chorales.

Bach, Wilhelm Friedemann (Germany, 1710–1784): Composer and keyboardist; eldest son of J. S. Bach; wrote numerous keyboard, instrumental, and choral works.

Bartók, Béla (Hungary, 1881–1945): Composer of string quartets, orchestral works, operas, and piano-teaching pieces; instrumental in collecting Hungarian folk music and incorporating it into his works.

Beethoven, Ludwig van (Germany, 1770–1827): Outstanding composer of the late eighteenth and early nineteenth centuries; his music represents the culmination of the Classic period and an important beginning to the Romantic period; composed nine symphonies, seventeen string quartets, thirty-two piano sonatas, an opera, piano concertos, and chamber music.

Berens, Hermann (Germany, 1826–1880): Composer of piano pieces, songs, chamber music and operas; pianist and professor at the Stockholm Conservatory.

Bielawa, Herbert (United States, b. 1930): Composer and professor emeritus of theory and composition at San Francisco State University; compositions include electronic works, chamber music, keyboard works (solo and ensemble), and a variety of vocal and instrumental pieces.

Biggs, John (United States, b. 1932): Southern California composer; chosen as composer-in-residence for six colleges in northeastern Kansas from 1967 to 1971; performs in his own John Biggs Consort throughout the world.

Brahms, Johannes (Germany, 1833–1897): Late Romantic period composer and pianist; master of the "variation" compositional device; wrote four symphonies, concertos, chamber music, choral works, songs, and keyboard pieces.

Brubeck, Dave (United States, b. 1920): One of the most notable musicians of the jazz era; his legendary quartet, the most popular combo of the fifties, was one of the first to issue live recordings of concerts.

Chopin, Frédéric (Poland, 1810–1849): One of the foremost keyboard composers of the early Romantic period; wrote many mazurkas, études, preludes, ballades, waltzes, polonaises, and fantasies, and two piano concertos.

Cohan, George M. (United States, 1878–1942): Composer, actor, producer, and playwright; wrote many musical comedies and popular songs, frequently with patriotic themes.

Czerny, Carl (Austria, 1791–1857): Pianist and pedagogue who composed symphonies, overtures, chamber music, and masses and other sacred music; known for his numerous collections of piano studies and exercises.

Denver, John (United States, b. 1943): Singer, composer, guitarist, environmentalist; received international recognition as composer of Peter, Paul, and Mary's hit "Leavin' on a Jet Plane"; other number one hits included "Sunshine on My Shoulders" and "Annie's Song."

Diabelli, Anton (Austria, 1781–1858): Viennese publisher and composer; composed a waltz theme on which Beethoven based his "Diabelli Variations."

Diemer, Emma Lou (United States, b. 1927): Professor of theory and composition at the University of California, Santa Barbara; compositions include works for orchestra and band, chamber ensemble, organ, piano, and chorus as well as solo songs and song cycles.

Dvořák, Antonín (Bohemia, 1841–1904): Composer who established a distinct Czech national music by including elements of Czech folk-song style in his works; compositions include operas, symphonic poems, chamber music, concertos, piano pieces, songs and symphonies; his most frequently performed work is the Symphony No. 9 (*From the New World*), which he composed during his stay in the United States (1892–1895).

Emerson, Ida (United States, late 19th–20th c.): Composer who collaborated on several songs with lyricist Joseph Howard.

Evans, Lee (United States, b. 1937): Pianist, composer, performer, and teacher; specializes in teaching a "classical" approach to jazz.

Finney, Ross Lee (United States, b. 1906): Composer of songs, piano and organ pieces, chamber music, choral works with orchestra, concertos, four symphonies, and other orchestral works.

Gurlitt, Cornelius (Germany, 1820–1901): Keyboardist, composer, and teacher who wrote operas, orchestral and choral works, chamber music, song cycles, and numerous piano pieces.

Handel, George Frideric (Germany, 1685–1759): Composer who, with J. S. Bach, represents the culmination of the late Baroque period; his works include many operas, oratorios (for example, *Messiah*), concertos, and chamber music.

Hanon, Charles Louis (France, 1820–1900): Writer of a collection of sixty technique exercises (*The Virtuoso Pianist*) that has become one of the standard technical keyboard works.

Haydn, Franz Joseph (Austria, 1732–1809): Oldest of the three leading composers of the Classic period (with Mozart and Beethoven); wrote 104 symphonies and 88 string quartets, as well as oratorios, choral music, operas, and keyboard music.

Hilton, John (England, 1599–1657): Composer and organist; wrote *Catch That Catch Can* (1652), a collection of catches, rounds, and canons.

Howard, Joseph E. (United States, 1878–1961): Composer-singer of early Broadway musicals who wrote the lyrics for several songs with composer Ida Emerson, one of which was the popular "Hello Ma' Baby."

Johnson, Tom (United States, b. 1939): Contemporary composer, pianist, writer, and music critic; much of his music, which reflects a "minimalist" attitude, explores visual and verbal, as well as musical, media.

Joplin, Scott (United States, 1868–1917): Composer and pianist known as the "King of Classic Ragtime"; in addition to his fifty or more piano pieces, he wrote songs, a ragtime ballet, and two operas.

Kabalevsky, Dmitri (Russia, 1904–1987): Composer who wrote operas, ballets, symphonies, incidental music for plays and films, as well as numerous piano pieces; in addition to composing, he became an important spokesperson on Soviet cultural policy, a teacher, and an administrator.

Köhler, Louis (Germany, 1820–1886): Composer of operas, orchestral and vocal works, and numerous piano studies; he also published a number of theoretical and pedagogical writings.

Kristofferson, Kris (United States, b. 1936): Vocalist, composer, guitarist, and actor whose country superstar image is a result of his classic songs "Me and Bobby McGee," "Help Me Make It Through the Night," "Sunday Morning Coming Down," and "For the Good Times."

Lennon, John (England, 1940–1980): Composer, vocalist, guitarist, and founding member of the number one recording group of all time, the Beatles; the Lennon/McCartney (fellow Beatle Paul McCartney) songwriting duo was one of popular music's most successful collaborations.

McCartney, Paul (England, b. 1942): Composer, vocalist, guitarist, bassist with legendary Beatles; collaborated with fellow Beatle John Lennon on most of the band's most popular songs.

Manone, Joseph ("Wingy") (United States, 1904–1982): Swing-era jazz trumpeter, with one arm; also a singer and bandleader; his "Tar Paper Stomp" became the hit "In the Mood" for Glenn Miller's band.

Martines, Marianne (Austria, 1744–1812): Vocalist, pianist, teacher, and composer; wrote oratorios, motets, psalms, symphonies, piano concertos, cantatas, masses, and keyboard sonatas; founded her own singing school, which she operated out of her home.

Morrison, Jim (United States, 1943–1971): Composer, vocalist, poet, and leader of the Doors, the Los Angeles–based rock group that he helped form in 1965; hit singles include "Light My Fire" and "Riders on the Storm."

Mozart, Leopold (Austria, 1719–1787): Composer, pianist, and father of Wolfgang Amadeus Mozart; wrote operas, oratorios, cantatas, masses and other sacred choral works, symphonies, concertos, and chamber music; compiled music books of keyboard pieces for his son and for his daughter, Nannerl.

Mozart, Wolfgang Amadeus (Austria, 1756–1791): With Haydn and Beethoven, one of the finest composers of the Viennese Classic period; a child prodigy, Mozart wrote a vast quantity of music, including keyboard pieces, operas, symphonies, concertos, chamber music, and choral music.

Müller, August Eberhard (Germany, 1787–1817): Conductor, flautist, keyboard player, pedagogue, and composer of concertos, keyboard and chamber music, and various vocal works.

Niebergall, Julia Lee (United States, 1886–1968): Pianist and ragtime composer who is known as one of the leaders in the development of Indianapolis ragtime; composed three rags.

Olson, Lynn Freeman (United States, 1938–1987): Composer, author of many piano books, and music educator; his work has appeared on several highly successful children's television shows.

Persichetti, Vincent (United States, 1915–1987): Composer of nine symphonies, orchestral works, concertos, an oratorio, choral and band works, chamber music, piano and organ pieces, and numerous songs; author of *Twentieth-Century Harmony.*

Rameau, Jean Philippe (France, 1683–1764): Composer, theorist, and organist; wrote numerous operas, chamber cantatas, canons, motets, and keyboard music.

Rebikov, Vladimir (Russia, 1866–1920): Composer whose early works were in the Romantic style, but about 1900 began writing expressionist dramatic and vocal pieces using whole-tone harmony and other contemporary idioms.

Sartorio, Arnoldo (Germany, 1853–?): Author of a piano method book and composer of numerous instructive piano pieces.

Scarlatti, Domenico (Italy, 1685–1757): Composer and harpsichordist who wrote hundreds of compositions for the harpsichord and is credited with innovations that led to the modern keyboard style.

Schubert, Franz (Austria, 1797–1828): One of the leading composers of early romanticism, his works include over six hundred songs, eight symphonies, piano works, chamber music, and music for the stage.

Schumann, Robert (Germany, 1810–1856): One of the most important of the many pianist-composers of the nineteenth century; wrote numerous songs and short piano pieces in addition to symphonies, concertos, and chamber music.

Shostakovich, Dmitri (Russia, 1906–1975): One of the leading symphonic composers of the twentieth century; wrote symphonies, operas, chamber music, and keyboard works.

Stravinsky, Igor (Russia, 1882–1971): An original and sometimes revolutionary composer of the twentieth century; wrote influential scores for ballets, orchestral works, and operas, and explored a wide variety of styles, including jazz and ragtime.

Szymanowska, Maria (Poland, 1789–1831): Acclaimed as one of the greatest women pianists of the nineteenth century and one of the first women composers of Poland; composed mainly piano character pieces: études, nocturnes, and mazurkas.

Türk, Daniel Gottlob (Germany, 1750–1813): Composer, violinist, organist, and teacher of the Classical period (Mozart and Haydn were his contemporaries); known for his keyboard pieces and the method book *Klavierschule.*

Valens, Ritchie (Richard Valenzuela; United States, 1941–1959): Guitarist, singer, songwriter; first Mexican-American Rock performer; his first hit single was "La Bamba" (sung in Spanish) and was based on the Spanish folk song of the same name.

Van de Vate, Nancy (United States, b. 1930): Composer of orchestral, chamber, vocal, and keyboard works; her music has been performed in eighteen countries on four continents; founder of the International League of Women Composers.

Vangelis (Vangelis Papathanassiau, Greece, 20th c.): Composer and keyboard player who first gained recognition as leader of the group Aphrodite's Child; won an Oscar for best score for the Oscar-winning movie *Chariots of Fire.*

Webber, Andrew Lloyd (England, b. 1948): Composer of the scores of numerous hit musicals and popular operas, notably *Jesus Christ Superstar, Cats,* and *Phantom of the Opera.*

GLOSSARY

A B A musical form consisting of two sections, A and B, that contrast with each other (binary).

A B A A musical form consisting of three sections, A B A. Two are the same and the middle one is different (ternary).

accent A stress or emphasis given to certain tones. An accent sign is >.

accidental A sign introduced before a note of a composition that changes the pitch for one measure only: ♯ (sharp), ♭ (flat), ♮ (natural).

accompaniment Music that goes with or provides harmonic or rhythmic support for another musical part (usually a melody).

Alberti bass A left-hand accompaniment (named after the eighteenth-century keyboard composer, Domenico Alberti) consisting of a figure of broken chords.

alla breve (¢) A term indicating two beats to a measure (duple meter); usually stands for ²⁄₂.

anacrusis (ana-CREW-sis) An unaccented beat, often the last beat of a measure.

arpeggio, arpeggiated A pattern in which every tone of the chord is played separately, one after the other.

asymmetric meter Meter in which the beat groupings are irregular, as ⁵⁄₄ or ⁷⁄₈. Often created by combining two meters: ²⁄₄ and ³⁄₄ = ⁵⁄₄.

atonal Twentieth-century music in which no tonic or key center is apparent.

augmented triad A three-note chord built with two major thirds.

authentic cadence A cadence in which the dominant chord (V) precedes the tonic (I).

bagatelle A short, light composition, usually for piano.

bar or bar line A vertical line through the staff to indicate a boundary for a measure of music.

Baroque period The period in music history spanning approximately the years 1600–1750.

bass clef The symbol ℭ, which determines that the fourth line of the staff is F below middle C.

beat The underlying steady pulse present in most music; the rhythmic unit to which one responds in marching or dancing.

beat groupings *See* **meter.**

binary form A musical form consisting of two sections, A and B, that contrast with each other.

bitonality The use of two different scales/tonalities simultaneously.

blue notes Notes that are lowered—usually the third and the seventh tones of a major scale; often used in popular music and jazz.

blues Sorrow songs created by African-Americans that influenced the development of jazz. Special characteristics include flatted third and seventh scale tones, the use of groups of twelve measures, seventh chords, syncopation, and improvisation.

blues scale A scale that can only be approximated in traditional notation or on the keyboard; a major scale with the third and the seventh pitches lowered a half step (the fifth is also lowered a half step in some bebop music).

boogie-woogie A jazz piano style (fast blues) in which the left hand repeats a fast-moving bass (generally moving through tonic, subdominant, and dominant harmonies) while the right hand improvises a melody part.

bourrée (BU-ray) A popular French dance of the Baroque period, in quick duple meter, with a short upbeat.

breve A note value that is equivalent to two whole notes, written as ⊟ or ▮◑▮ .

cadence A point of arrival that punctuates a musical phrase, section, and composition.

canon A musical form in which all parts have the same melody throughout but start at different times. A round is a type of canon.

celesta A percussion instrument in the form of a small upright piano; its tone is produced by the striking of steel bars with hammers connected to a keyboard by a simplified piano action.

chamber music Music played by small groups such as a piano trio or a string quartet.

chorale Hymn tune.

chord A combination of three or more pitches a third apart, sounded together.

chord progression A series of chords sounding in succession.

chord root The pitch on which a chord is constructed; the most important pitch in the chord.

chord tones The individual pitches within a chord.

chromatic scale A twelve-tone scale consisting entirely of half steps.

circle of fifths The key signatures of the major and minor keys arranged in a circular sequence of perfect fifths.

classical music A term for art music of Western European civilization, usually created by a trained composer.

Classic period The period in music history spanning approximately the years 1750–1820.

clavichord A stringed keyboard instrument used from the fifteenth through the eighteenth centuries; instead of hammers striking the strings as on a piano, tangents (upright metal wedges) strike the strings.

clef A symbol placed on a staff to designate a precise pitch that identifies the other pitches in the score.

compound meter A grouping of beats (meter) in which the beat is divided into three equal parts.

Contemporary period The period in music that is current.

continuo Abbreviation for basso continuo; the continuous bass part that was performed by the harpsichord or organ in works of the Baroque period and served as the basis for harmonies.

contour The shape of a melodic line.

contrary motion A type of motion in which two or more parts move in opposite directions.

damper pedal The piano pedal to the far right that, when pressed down, releases the dampers from the strings and allows the strings to vibrate freely, sustaining the sound; generally, used to produce a legato effect.

diatonic A seven-tone scale, consisting of five whole steps and two half steps, utilizing every pitch name. Major and minor scales are diatonic scales.

diminished triad A three-note chord built with two minor thirds.

dominant The fifth tone or chord of a major or minor scale.

dominant seventh chord A four-note chord constructed on the fifth degree of the scale with a minor seventh added above the root.

double flat A symbol that indicates that the written pitch is to be lowered two half steps: ♭♭.

double sharp A symbol that indicates that the written pitch is to be raised two half steps: ✕.

downbeat The first beat of a measure, usually accented.

drone An accompaniment created by sounding one or more tones (usually two, five notes apart) simultaneously and continuously throughout a composition or section of a composition; a special type of harmony.

duet A composition written for two performers.

duple meter A grouping of beats (meter) into two ($\frac{2}{4}$, $\frac{2}{2}$).

duration The length of time a musical tone sounds.

dynamics The degree and range of loudness of musical sounds.

electronic music Music made by creating, altering, and imitating sounds electronically.

enharmonic tones Tones sounding the same pitch or key on the keyboard but written differently, as E-flat and D-sharp.

étude French word meaning "study"; a technical study designed to facilitate technique.

expressionism A musical style of the early twentieth century in which irregular rhythms, jagged melody lines, and dissonances were used to express strong subjective feelings.

flat A symbol that indicates that the written pitch is to be lowered a half step: ♭.

folk song A song having no known composer, usually transmitted orally, and reflecting the musical consensus of a cultural group.

form The plan, order or design in which a piece of music is organized, incorporating repetition and contrast.

gavotte A French dance in moderately quick duple meter, often with an upbeat of two quarter notes.

glissando A very rapid sliding passage up or down the white and black keys.

grace note A short note, printed in small type, that ornaments the note that follows it. A grace note is not counted in the rhythm of the measure.

grand or **great staff** Treble and bass clef staves joined together by a vertical line and a bracket.

half step An interval comprising two adjacent pitches, as C to C♯.

harmonic minor scale A minor scale in which the pattern of whole and half steps is: whole, half, whole, whole, half, whole & half, half.

harmony A simultaneous sounding of two or more tones.

harpsichord A keyboard instrument, popular in the Renaissance and Baroque periods; instead of hammers striking the strings as on a piano, the strings are plucked by quills.

homophonic A musical texture in which all parts move in the same rhythm but use different pitches, as in hymns; also, a melody supported by chords.

hymn A religious song; usually a metric poem to be sung by a congregation.

imitation The restatement of a theme in different voices (parts).

impressionism A musical style of the late nineteenth and early twentieth centuries, in which musical textures and timbres were used to convey impressions (hint) rather than make precise "statements."

improvisation Music performed extemporaneously, often within a framework determined by the musical style.

indeterminate music "Chance" music emphasizing improvisation within limitations set by the composer.

interval The distance between two tones, named by counting all pitch names involved; a harmonic interval occurs when two pitches are sounded simultaneously, and a melodic interval occurs when two pitches are sounded successively.

inversion The rearrangement of the pitches of a chord, for example, CEG becomes GCE; performing a melody by turning the contour upside down.

jazz A style that originated with African-Americans in the early twentieth century, characterized by improvisation and syncopated rhythms.

key The scale and tonality of a composition.

key signature The sharps or the flats at the beginning of the staff, after the clef sign, indicating in which key or on what scale the composition is written.

leading tone The seventh tone or triad of a major or a harmonic or melodic minor scale.

leger or **ledger lines** (LEH-jer) Short lines above or below the five-line staff on which higher or lower pitches may be indicated.

major interval An interval a half step larger than the corresponding minor interval.

major scale A scale in which the pattern of whole and half steps is: whole, whole, half, whole, whole, whole, half.

major triad A three-note chord with a major third and a minor third.

march A composition written in duple meter with a strong, vigorous rhythm and regular phrases.

mazurka A Polish dance in quick triple meter with strong emphasis on beat 2 or 3.

measure A unit of beats delineated by bar lines; informally called a "bar."

mediant The third tone or triad of a major or minor scale.

Medieval period Also called Middle Ages; the earliest period in Western music history, spanning approximately the years 500–1420.

melodic minor scale A minor scale in which the ascending pattern of whole and half steps is: whole, half, whole, whole, whole, whole, half, whereas the descending pattern is identical with the natural minor scale.

melodic rhythm Durations of pitches used in a melody.

melody A succession of sounds (pitches) and silences moving one at a time through time.

meter The grouping of beats in music.

meter signature Two numerals that show the number of beats grouped in a measure and the basic beat: $\frac{3}{4}$.

middle C The C midway between the treble and bass clefs; approximately midway on the piano keyboard.

minimalism A twentieth-century musical style in which the musical elements are subjected to a minimal amount of development; an attempt to simplify music by using the fewest of means.

minor interval An interval a half step smaller than the corresponding major interval.

minor scale A scale in which one characteristic feature is a half step between the second and third tones. There are three forms of minor scales: natural, harmonic, and melodic.

minor triad A three-note chord that includes a minor third and a major third.

minuet A dance in triple meter with an elegant, graceful quality of movement; of French origin.

modes Scales (each with seven notes) consisting of various patterns of whole and half steps. The seven possible modes—Ionian, Dorian, Phrygian, Lydian, Mixolydian, Aeolian, and Locrian—were used in the Medieval and Renaissance periods and served as the basis from which major and minor scales emerged.

modulation The change from one key to another within a composition.

monophonic A musical texture created when a single melody is heard without accompaniment.

motive A brief rhythmic or melodic figure that recurs throughout a composition as a unifying element.

musical style The characteristic manner in which the musical elements—melody, rhythm, harmony, and form—are treated in a piece of music.

natural A sign that cancels a sharp or a flat: ♮. A note that is neither sharp nor flat, as C, D, E, F, G, A, B on the piano keyboard.

natural minor scale A minor scale in which the pattern of whole and half steps is: whole, half, whole, whole, half, whole, whole.

neighboring tones Tones placed a step above (upper neighbor) or a step below (lower neighbor) two repeated pitches.

oblique motion A type of motion in which one part remains stationary while the other parts move.

octave The interval in which two pitches share the same letter name (C-C) and are eight steps apart (eight lines and spaces from one note to the next); one pitch with twice the frequency of the other.

opus (op.) A composition or group of compositions with designated numbers that indicate the chronological position of the composition(s) in the composer's total output.

organ A keyboard wind instrument consisting of a series of pipes standing on a wind chest; features one or more keyboards, operated by a player's hands and feet. The portative organ was a small portable organ of the late Middle Ages while the positive organ was a self-contained, medium-sized organ also used in the Middle Ages.

ostinato A continuous repetition of a melodic or rhythmic pattern.

parallel keys The major and minor scales that share the same tonic but have different key signatures.

parallel motion A type of motion in which two or more parts move in the same direction.

passing tones Tones placed stepwise between chord tones.

pattern *See* **motive.**

pedals Levers operated by the feet on pianos and organs; pianos have a damper pedal, a sostenuto pedal, and an una corda pedal.

pentatonic scale A five-tone scale often identified with the pattern of the black keys of the piano. Many other five-tone arrangements are possible.

phrase A musical segment with a clear beginning and ending, comparable to a simple sentence or a clause in speech.

plagal cadence A cadence in which the subdominant chord (IV) precedes the tonic (I).

polyphonic A musical texture created when two or more melodies sound simultaneously.

polytonal Music that employs two or more tonalities (or keys) simultaneously.

prelude An introductory piece for a larger composition or drama, usually written for a solo instrument; in the nineteenth century "Prelude" was used as the title for piano character pieces.

primary chords The three chords built on the first degree (I), the fourth degree (IV), and the fifth degree (V) of any major or harmonic or melodic minor scale.

quadruple meter A grouping of beats into four ($\frac{4}{4}$, $\frac{4}{8}$, $\frac{4}{2}$).

ragtime Piano music, developed at the turn of the century, that features a syncopated melody against a steady "oom PAH" bass; piano "rags" are usually divided into three or four different sections—each symmetrical in length.

relative keys The major and minor scales that share the same key signature but different tonics.

Renaissance period The period in Western music history spanning approximately the years 1420–1600.

rest A symbol designating silence.

retrograde Backward motion; beginning with the last note of a melody and ending with the first.

rhythm All of the duration or lengths of sounds and silences that occur in music; the organization of sounds and silences in time.

rhythm of the melody *See* **melodic rhythm.**

rhythm pattern Any grouping, generally brief, of long and short sounds and silences.

Romantic period The period in Western music history spanning approximately the years 1820–1900.

rondo A musical form consisting of a recurring section with two or more contrasting sections, as A B A C A.

root The tone on which a chord is built. A chord using C as its root is labeled a C chord.

round A melody performed by two or more groups entering at stated and different times; also called "canon."

scale A pattern of pitches arranged in ascending or descending order. Scales are identified by their specific arrangement of whole and half steps. *See also* **major scale; minor scale; chromatic scale; pentatonic scale; whole-tone scale.**

secondary chords The four chords built on the second degree (II), the third degree (III), the sixth degree (VI), and the seventh degree (VII) of any major or harmonic or melodic minor scale.

section A distinct portion of a composition; one of a number of parts that together make a composition. A section consists of several phrases.

serial music Music that uses a set sequence of pitches as the basis for a composition, such as arranging the twelve pitches of the chromatic scale into a series and then manipulating that series.

seventh chord A four-note chord built in thirds.

sharp A symbol that raises the pitch a half step ($\sharp$).

shifting meter The changing of beat groupings in music, as from twos to threes.

simple meter A grouping of beats (meter) in which the beat is divided into two equal parts.

skip A melodic interval exceeding a second or whole step.

slur A curved line, above or below a number of notes, that indicates that these pitches should be connected (legato).

sonata An extended composition in several movements for one to two instruments.

sonata form The most important form of the Classic period; includes a main theme and a subsidiary theme presented in the *exposition*, followed by a *development* of the themes, and concludes with a restatement, or *recapitulation*, of the themes.

sostenuto pedal The piano pedal in the middle that, when depressed, sustains only those tones whose dampers are already raised by the action of the keys.

step An interval of a second, as A to B.

subdominant The fourth tone or triad of a major or minor scale.

submediant The sixth tone or triad of a major or minor scale.

subtonic The seventh tone of a natural minor scale.

supertonic The second tone or triad of a major or minor scale.

syncopation Placement of emphasis on normally weak beats or weak parts of beats.

tempo The rate of speed of music.

ternary form A musical form consisting of three sections, A B A; two are the same and the middle one is different.

tetrachord Four successive scale tones.

theme A distinctive melodic statement, usually part of a long movement.

theme and variations A composition in which each section is a modified version of the original musical theme.

tie A curved line that connects two identical notes and indicates that they should be performed as a single note; to perform, strike the first note only and hold through the time value of the second:

timbre The quality or color of sound; the characteristic sound of an instrument. Synonyms: tone color, tone quality.

time Commonly used in place of more precise terms, namely, meter, rhythm, tempo, duration.

time signature *See* **meter signature.**

tonality The relationship of tones in a scale to the tonic.

tonal music Music that is centered on a particular tonic or key center.

tone cluster The simultaneous sounding of a group of adjacent tones, usually dissonant in sound.

tone row A series of twelve tones (the tones of a chromatic scale), arranged in a specific order, that forms the basis for a musical composition.

tonic The central tone or chord of the key and the first note or chord of a major or minor scale.

transposition Changing a piece of music from one key (scale/tonality) to another.

treble clef The symbol 𝄞, which determines the second line of the staff as G above middle C.

triad A three-note chord with pitches a third apart.

triple meter A grouping of beats (meter) into threes ($\frac{3}{4}$, $\frac{3}{8}$, $\frac{3}{2}$).

twelve-tone row *See* **tone row.**

una corda pedal The piano pedal to the far left that, when depressed, shifts the grand piano keyboard so that each hammer strikes only two of the three strings in the upper register and only one in the lower; the same effect of reducing the volume is achieved by different means on an upright piano.

upbeat *See* **anacrusis.**

virginal A small type of harpsichord with one set of strings and jacks and one keyboard; the earliest forms were shaped like a rectangular box and placed on a table or held in the performer's lap.

Western art music Art music of Western European civilization, usually created by a trained composer.

whole step An interval comprising two consecutive half steps, as C to D.

whole-tone scale A scale of six different tones, each a whole step apart.

CLASSIFIED INDEXES

Ensemble Pieces

Technique Exercises

Composing Projects

INDEX OF TITLES

SUBJECT INDEX